To: Dorothy.

With best wishes

Charlie

Cambridge

19 June 2024

Malacca Strait to River Cam

- a memoir -

By Y.W. Loke

Cam Rivers Publishing

First English Edition Published in Great Britain

By CAM RIVERS PUBLISHING LTD 2024

MALACCA STRAIT TO RIVER CAM
- A MEMOIR -

Author: Y.W. Loke

Honorary Editor: Professor Alan Macfarlane FBA
Editor-in-Chief: WANG Zilan
Editors: Irene Galstian, Levente Koroes, QIN Yuchen, Oliver Hargrave

Cover Design: GE Dalong (MUYE)
The painting on the front cover: David Paskett
The portrait on page 56 was painted by Anna Paik
Design and Typeset: QIN Yubin (MUYE) and Irene Galstian
The black-and-white photograph on the back cover: Tao Keng Beng

The publishing of this book is supported by
the Vanishing Worlds Foundation, U.K.

A CIP Catalogue of this book is available from the British Library

ISBN: 978-1-916858-32-9

Contact: press@cambridgerivers.com
www.cambridgerivers.com

The Author

Yung Wai (Charlie) Loke was born in Kuala Lumpur, Malaysia. He spent his early childhood in Penang, an island off the west coast of the Malay Peninsula. After boarding school in England, he graduated from Cambridge University (MA) and holds doctorates in both Medicine (MD) and Science (ScD). He is Honorary Fellow of the Royal College of Obstetricians and Gynaecologists (FRCOG) in recognition of the contributions his research has made to these clinical specialties. He is Professor Emeritus of Reproductive Immunology at the University of Cambridge and Fellow of King's College Cambridge. He presently lives in Cambridge but retains a home in Malaysia where he hopes to return one day.

Synopsis

My memoir spans 80 years from the Japanese occupation of Malaya during World War II to the present COVID-19 pandemic in Britain. It tells the story of how a boy from a far-off tropical island in the Andaman Sea became a don in Cambridge University and began a life in scientific research. The chapters (as listed in the table of contents) describe the journey.

For Penny, Tracey, Amanda, Tamsin and Imogen.

CONTENTS

Prologue

Cambridge, May 1964

'Now that you have gained your doctorate, what are your future plans?' Professor Kendal Dixon asked me. 'There is a position for a demonstrator coming up in the University Department of Pathology. Would you like to apply?' he added.

We were dining together in King's College. Kendal taught me when I was an undergraduate there in the early 1950s. This was the first time I've been back since graduation. Earlier that day, I had successfully defended my thesis for the degree of Doctor of Medicine.

I remember this conversation vividly because it marked the beginning of my journey 'from Malacca Strait to River Cam'.

I thought about it throughout the flight home to Malaysia. By the time we landed, I had made up my mind. Yes, I would apply. The tenure of a Demonstrator is for 3 years in the first instance with the possibility of a further 2-year extension. To spend 3–5 years teaching in Cambridge would be a fascinating experience. After having been an undergraduate in the University, it would be a pleasant change to sample life on the other side as a don. Back to familiar turf, but this time without the torment of Tripos examinations every summer. I would be setting exam questions instead of answering them. It should be fun, a temporary interlude before returning home to Malaysia. I never thought of it as a permanent career move, as it turned out to be.

Much of my life was unplanned. Things just happened, through a combination of luck, chance and serendipity.

While waiting to defend my thesis, I had enrolled for a diploma course at the London School of Hygiene and Tropical Medicine to learn about parasites and the diseases they cause. Living in the tropics, I have been enthralled by these exotic creatures with their exquisite life-cycles, like beautiful works of art.

By a happy coincidence, the Department of Pathology in Cambridge was at that time in the process of reorganising their teaching in parasitology and looking for someone who could contribute to this area. The diploma in tropical medicine

(DTM&H) became a useful addition to my newly acquired MD degree in my CV for the Cambridge application. Luck was on my side. My application was successful. I was duly appointed as Demonstrator in the Department of Pathology to start in the academic year of October 1967.

We decided to travel to the UK by boat as we had a lot of luggage for our new life. This would be the second voyage for Penny and me but this time in the reverse direction. The first, in 1960, was as a married couple. Now we were accompanied by three children aged 6, 4 and 2. On reflection, I think we were either very brave or just foolish to have embarked on such an adventure with two young children and a toddler in tow. Fortunately, Penny, as always, was very organised and unfazed by it all.

We set sail from the island of Penang in the summer of 1967. The voyage took over 5 weeks because the Suez Canal was closed due to the conflict there. I remember the day we rounded the notorious Cape of Good Hope in South Africa. It was 19 September, our eldest daughter Tracey's 6th birthday. The ship had organised a children's party and Dad had to be there to cut the cake. I am a very bad sailor who can be seasick even in the calmest conditions. That day, the waves were enormous. I could hardly stand up, the ship was pitching and rolling so badly. But I managed to do my paternal duties.

It was a great relief to finally set foot on dry land again. We were a bit late arriving in Cambridge. I missed the first two weeks of the Michaelmas term.

That was how my life in Cambridge began. There was the sense of a new beginning. I had entered a scholastic world with its own customs and traditions. It even has its own rhythm. My university diary, for example, runs from October to October to coincide with the academic rather than the calendar year. University life is largely separate from that of the city. It is a world within a world, a serene protected space.

I had arrived at a vital crossroads and had chosen the path I wished to follow. An academic life suits me. What I do sits comfortably with who I am. 'Every man's work is always a portrait of himself,' observes Samuel Butler.

1. Between Two Worlds

An academic life is not the career trajectory my parents have mapped out for me. I was expected to take over the reins of the family business and build on grandfather's legacy. My grandfather, Loke Yew, came from China in the early 19th century to what was then known as the Malay Archipelago as a penniless young man and made a fortune in tin and rubber. This is the 'rags-to-riches' chapter of the family history. His life has been told many times over. The most recent is *Loke Yew: A Malayan Pioneer* by Neil Khor published in 2019. Roads and buildings are named after him in many Asian cities. He had even issued his own currency which was legal tender.

Loke Yew died from malaria in 1917, aged 71. The cause of death in itself tells me much about his life. I can picture the harsh, mosquito-infested tropical jungle where he had toiled to establish his tin mines and rubber estates. Besides the scourge of diseases, it was also a turbulent period with no established law and order. Only those with a resilient pioneering spirit survived. We, his descendants, sitting in our comfortable homes, are now enjoying the fruits of his labour.

The infrastructure of the family office and staff was already in place waiting for me. All I had to do was to move in and join the firm. I could have easily slipped into a lotus-eating lifestyle. Instead, to everyone's surprise, I abandoned the business world for a life in academia. I have torn up the script intended for me and rewritten my own story. No members of the Loke clan have taken this up as a profession.

Yet, Loke Yew himself was a great supporter of scholarship. He was convinced that education was the key to a better life. He was one of the founders of Hong Kong University and received an Honorary Doctorate there in 1917. In recognition of his contribution, the University renamed its Great Hall as Loke Yew Hall in 1956. A bronze bust of Loke Yew now stands proudly at its entrance. I think my grandfather would approve of my career choice.

My decision not to join the family business was not an act of

Private currency issued by Loke Yew

rebellion, although some might have considered it to be a dereliction of duty and are disappointed I haven't used my wealth to create more wealth.

After all, that is how dynasties are founded. Perhaps, being born into wealth had dulled my hunger for more. At least I cannot be accused of being the feckless son who frittered away the family fortune. It is often said that private wealth seldom lasts beyond three generations.

My sister Ruby took over the running of the family company. She is a lawyer and much more suitable for that role than I can ever be. Under her guidance, our family wealth, originally created by our grandfather, remains securely intact.

We are lucky in that there are only three of us. Unlike the TV

Bronze bust of Loke Yew at the entrance of Loke Yew Hall, Hong Kong University

Vice-Chancellor of Hong Kong University gifting me a miniature model of Loke Yew Hall

drama *Succession* where siblings fight over control of the family company, our relationships are harmonious. My eldest sister Peggy lives in Canada and is not interested in the family business. I have voluntarily relinquished my position. So far, no hidden step-siblings have come out of the woodwork to lay claim to their right of succession.

I am very grateful to have support from family funding. It allowed me to chase my dream. Academia is intellectually exciting but financially unrewarding. Inherited wealth is often regarded as somewhat unfair. But it is part of life's lottery. Some people are born clever, others are talented or good looking. These other forms of privilege are just as important in determining life's success. Beauty alone can go a long way. As the dairymaid in the nursery rhyme 'My Pretty Maid' proudly declares, 'My face is my fortune.' We see this in the world of celebrities.

My original plan was to stay in Cambridge for the duration of my 3–5-year tenure and then return home to Malaysia. Instead, I have stayed for over 50 years and I am still here.

Why have I lingered so long in Cambridge? What is so special about the place? The answer is more elusive than I had expected because many of the things that spring to mind are not easily quantifiable.

Certainly, the sheer splendour of the surroundings can cast a hypnotic spell. But more than the environment is the intellectual community within. The days of a solitary genius like Isaac Newton making a scientific breakthrough from a eureka moment are long gone. Significant advances can only come about from team work. It is a slow progression through small incremental steps involving multiple researchers.

In Cambridge, there are ample opportunities for collaboration. If you need advice, all you have to do is to pick up the telephone, or, nowadays, send an e-mail and there will be an expert at the other end. This is why I decided to stay on in Cambridge. There are many scientists here whose expertise I can tap. I don't think I would have been able to do high quality research if I had returned home to Malaysia. I cannot deny there is also a tinge of pride in being a faculty member in one of the world's premier universities. I wouldn't have stayed on for so long if my life followed the same pattern as that of Jim Dixon, the protagonist in Kingsley Amis's campus novel *Lucky Jim*, who was described as a 'second-rate lecturer in a fourth-rate university'.

The subject of my research interest is the placenta, the organ which links the baby to its mother in the womb throughout pregnancy. By a remarkable coincidence, I see parallels in my own life and that of my research subject. During pregnancy, the placenta occupies a position midway between baby and mother inside the womb, in a kind of no-man's land, but is intimately connected to both. It has adapted itself to live between these two genetically distinct individuals. I, too, have adapted to live in the two contrasting worlds of Malaysia and Britain.

Here is a passage extracted from my profile published appropriately in the international scientific journal *Placenta* on the occasion of my retirement in 2002.

> Buffered between England and Malaysia yet intrinsic to neither country—he is not a British citizen despite having lived in Cambridge for more than 50 years and inhabiting a Georgian manor. He is as happy in a sarong, a tweed jacket or his scarlet academic gown, an anglicised foreigner or a foreign Englishman.

Yes, I am an anglicised foreigner but I am emphatically *not* a foreign Englishman. The former is to adapt. The latter is pretending to be somebody I am not. I cannot be English but I can try to blend in. There is a subtle difference between the two and I have always been careful not to cross the fine line.

How we see ourselves is just as important as how others see us. This self-awareness is a very important lesson I have learnt and it has served me well.

Self-awareness is equally important for the placenta. Indeed, it is crucial for its proper development. Both parents contribute to the placenta's heritage. Half its genes come from the mother and the other half from the father. To the mother, the placenta is, therefore, part 'self' (her own genes) and part 'non-self' (father's genes). The presence of her own genes allows the mother to accept the placenta as part of herself and not reject it as an alien invader.

But there are occasions when her own genes are not present in the placenta. This is when the egg used for conception is from a donor or when pregnancy takes place in a surrogate. Here, the maternal genes are from a third party and not from the mother carrying the baby. She no longer has the comfortable feeling that the placenta is part of herself. Immunologists have coined the term 'missing self' for such a situation. Lacking 'self' identity, these pregnancies are prone to many disorders. From the mother's perspective, the placenta can, therefore, be 'self', 'non-self' or 'missing self'. Pregnancy outcome will depend on how successful she is in coping with her placenta's myriad personalities.

Despite all the years I have spent in Britain, I have not surrendered my Malaysian passport. To me, it is not just a travel document. It is my identity and my sense of 'self'. It reminds me of who I am and keeps me grounded. After so long in the UK, I have subconsciously absorbed the habits, mannerisms and behaviour of the people around me. I sometimes forget I am a foreigner.

But there is a cost to being a cultural hybrid. It invites accusations that one is an impostor, an Oriental with a Western mindset who has betrayed his origin. Such an individual is often described with derision as a 'coconut' or a 'banana'—brown or yellow outside but white inside. But I would like to think that I have benefitted from two cultures rather than having lost my own.

The irony is that I had already been a cultural hybrid long before I even set foot in England. My mother's family are Peranakan or Straits Chinese from Penang. They are the present-day descendants of Chinese traders who sailed to the Malay Peninsula as far back as the 17th century, using the sea route between China and the West.

Many settled down in the ports along the way and married local women, resulting in a mixed heritage of customs and cultures, eventually becoming a distinct community. My maternal grandmother's daily attire, for example, is a *sarong kebaya,* which is a Malay costume rather than Chinese. Today, the ports of Penang, Malacca and Singapore are where large Peranakan communities are to be found. *Peranakan* is a Malay term meaning 'person born here'. The men are called *babas* and the women *nyonyas*. In *The Straits Chinese: A Cultural History*, author Khoo Joo Ee gives us a sweeping view of these communities.

I have been selfish following my own agenda without stopping to think how this might affect the rest of the family. My children, after so long in Britain, have largely lost touch with their Asian heritage. Amanda is the only daughter who lives in Asia. The others are all here in England. Penny, my wife, although English, is never entirely comfortable in the hothouse academic environment of university life. She admits she feels a bit lost and excluded. 'Even the cleaning lady seems to have a PhD!' she once exclaimed ruefully. She was happier living in Malaysia.

Many people have said to me, 'Why didn't you go back to Malaysia and help the country with your expertise?' Indeed, Prime Minister Dr Mahathir himself posed the same question to me when he visited Cambridge on 6 October 2000.

'Will you give me a job?' I asked him.

'I do not have that power,' he said with a smile.

If I were a surgeon or a physician, I could be quite useful as an extra pair of hands in the medical workforce. I know many clinicians who have returned, usually into private practice. But I am a research scientist working mainly in the laboratory. I need a team and a community of like-minded individuals. I will be lost working in a vacuum.

I did try, though. I once wrote to the University of Malaya

My mother

asking them if I could help to set up some research programme within the medical school. After sending in my CV, as requested, I heard nothing more, not even an acknowledgement. I detect an undercurrent of suspicion directed at overseas graduates returning home. Perhaps there is the fear that we might upset the cosy status quo.

I recently read about the experience of Wasim Khan. Although born in Britain, he has been absorbed by Pakistani cricket. So when he was offered the opportunity to run Pakistan's Cricket Board, he jumped at the chance. The decision to take the job was both professional and personal. He thought he would be going 'home' to help 'his own people'.

But he did not anticipate the hostility he faced. Because of his background, he was accused of not being Pakistani enough, that he was an import from a foreign country to do a job that should be reserved for a true Pakistani. While 'going home' to help is a laudable sentiment, there are unexpected obstacles along the way.

During my time in Cambridge, I've had many opportunities to move elsewhere. The only offer I had considered seriously was by Hong Kong University in 1982 who wanted me to head their Department of Pathology.

I was tempted. It would give me a reason to return to Asia. And also, my grandfather Loke Yew was one of the founders of the University. I gave it a great deal of thought but in the end decided not to go. To give up everything I have established in Cambridge was too much of a sacrifice. Besides, as Head of Department in HKU, I would be taking on more administrative duties, something I prefer to avoid. I sometimes wonder if I had made the right decision. This is not a statement of regret but just a question of what if and what might have been. I know Penny was disappointed with my decision. She loves Hong Kong.

Looking back now, the memory that haunts me is not returning to Malaysia earlier to look after my mother who was abandoned to live alone in our large family house in Kuala Lumpur. She survived my father by almost 30 years.

My mother died on 24 July 2006, aged 92. I just managed to get back to Kuala Lumpur in time to hold her hand as she passed away but I don't think she was aware of my presence. She was cremated and her ashes scattered over the sea at Port Dickson in an area as near as possible to the spot where we dispersed my father's ashes. At least I was there to perform this symbolic task. My father died on 11 November 1977 aged 72 from lung cancer.

In the relentless pursuit of my academic career, I have neglected more important duties. It is too late now to make amends. All I can do is to set the record straight and acknowledge this shameful act of neglect. There are other areas of my personal life that I am not proud of and memories I would rather forget. I cannot undo the pain I have caused except to say sorry to all those I have hurt.

'Regrets, I've had a few. But then again, too few to mention,' sings Frank Sinatra in 'My Way'. My own regrets are not so much about what I have done but rather what I have failed to do—journeys not taken; friendships neglected; loved ones abandoned; words unspoken. I didn't have the courage to seize the day as happened to butler Stevens, the protagonist in Kazuo Ishiguro's *Remains of the Day* when he realises too late that he had the opportunity to find love but let it slip by.

2. World War II

'Come back to the house at once. We are leaving!' I was happily fishing on the beach when I heard the frantic call. We were on holiday at Port Dickson, a seaside resort 60 miles from the capital Kuala Lumpur (KL) where we lived. We had a holiday house there. Back in those days, a family like ours will be accompanied by the whole household whenever we go on holiday, including cook, servants, *amahs* (nannies) and chauffeurs. I had no idea why we were suddenly cutting our stay short. When I got back to the house, I found everyone busily packing. From their anxious faces, I knew something was wrong.

The news came through that Japan had entered World War II when they signed the Tripartite Pact with Nazi Germany and Fascist Italy. Previously it was Europe's war but now Asia became involved. The year was 1941. I was 7 years old.

The stable and comfortable life of the pre-war era was soon to be replaced by one of fear and foreboding during the Japanese occupation. My world was turned upside down. Everything we once took for granted was swept away. No matter how extensively a country is destroyed in war time, life can never be as harrowing as living under occupation by a foreign power, especially a brutal one. There was a constant, corrosive anxiety.

When rumours circulated that the Japanese army was about to invade Malaya, our family fled to Singapore which was deemed to be impregnable. History tells a different story. The big guns of Singapore were all pointing towards the sea from where the Japanese invasion was presumed to materialise. Instead, the Japanese infantry traversed Malaya, besieging Singapore from the North. In no time, Singapore fell.

The Japanese army entered Singapore on 15 February 1942, a fateful date deeply etched into the minds of everyone who was there at that time. Even today, there are still some people here who refuse to have anything to do with the Japanese community. I cannot remember much of what happened immediately afterwards, either because I was too young or maybe I had simply blocked it from my memory.

It was while watching the television drama *The Singapore Grip*, based on the novel by J.G. Farrell about the fall of Singapore, that a vague picture began to emerge. In the chaotic days before the Japanese entered Singapore, there was a mad rush to get on a boat (any boat) to escape. But first, we had to obtain exit permits to leave Singapore. Europeans were given priority. My parents' application was too late and we missed the last boat out. It must have been a harrowing experience for my parents with three small children in tow trying frantically to get the family away to safety.

My Uncle Loke Wan Tho (discussed further in chapter 5) managed to secure a berth on the *Nova Moller* and made it to India. But only just. The ship was sunk by a Japanese air attack. Many drowned but my uncle was one of the lucky ones who was rescued from the water with severe burns. My grandmother, a devout Buddhist, consulted her favourite Goddess of Mercy who warned her: "Do not get on that boat. It is cursed!" Believers will nod wisely while sceptics will claim it is nothing more than just coincidence.

Fate can play cruel tricks. After riding out the storm in the war, Uncle Wan Tho and his wife Mavis were killed in a plane crash on 20th June 1964 while making a peacetime commercial flight from Singapore to Taiwan. He was 49. The official investigation blamed engine failure compounded by pilot error. But there are many conspiracy theories like sabotage, a hijack attempt that went wrong or the plane was simply overloaded. We shall never know the true reason why Flight 106 carrying delegates to the 11th Asian Film Festival never made it.

Of all my relatives, Uncle Wan Tho would have been the one to empathise with the life I have chosen. I wrote to him often when I was at school in Penang before I left for England. The executors of his estate found several of my letters and thoughtfully returned them to me.

Here is an excerpt from one dated 2 October 1947 with a heartfelt message:

> We missed you very much since the day you went home. It was so nice when you were here. We are now

Uncle Wan Tho with me, Peggy, and Ruby on King's Bridge

> very lonely. We have another reason for being sad when you went home and that is we have nobody to talk with. Most of the people who came and lived in our house do not want to talk with us except you who will talk and play with us. When are you coming to Penang again?

In other letters, I would include snippets of news about myself:

> I am glad to tell you I am the 2nd boy in the class this term and received a beautiful certificate of merit. In the school tennis tournament, I lost in the finals in the singles and doubles but I am satisfied for becoming the runner up in both. I got a small cup for the singles and a medal for the doubles.

The letter that made me laugh out loud when I read it was about a visit to the opera:

> Brother Michael, our orchestra conductor, invited all the member [*sic*] of the orchestra to the show, *Barber of Seville*. I hope you don't mind my saying that it was the worst show I have ever seen. There were so few people in the theatre that you could count them on your fingurs [*sic*]. Every time it's singing and to make it worse it's Italian. We couldn't understand a word. One of the Brothers, who is an Italian, laughed and clapped his hands while we were sitting down trying to figure out what is the joke. We said to him, 'It's Greek to us', but he said, 'It's Italian to me'. We waited patiently till it was all over and sometimes laughing when there is nothing to laugh about. Anyway it was an interesting experience for I have not seen any pictures like that before. If that is the way they act in operas, I don't think I'll like them.

A thoroughly honest account, leaving no doubt as to how I felt.

The Japanese authorities decided to repatriate all Malayan citizens back to Malaya. We were loaded onto open air cattle trucks like those used to transport livestock. It was dark, cold and wet. I don't remember how long the journey took but it seemed interminable. The distance from Singapore to the Malayan capital is 250 miles.

When we arrived, there was pandemonium in the station with Japanese soldiers barking orders that no-one understood. My parents held us very tightly in case we became separated in the melee. Somehow or other, we managed to get through the crowds and out of the station. Since then, even after all these years, I always have a feeling of unease whenever I visit that railway station.

Life during the Japanese occupation was harsh. We were told always to bow to a Japanese soldier. Failure to do so could be met with a sharp slap to the face or worse, depending on the soldier's mood. Lamp posts on certain roads were festooned with the severed heads of executed prisoners as a deterrent to potential troublemakers.

Food was scarce, mostly reserved for Japanese troops. Tapioca roots replaced rice as our staple fare. *Ikan bilis*, tiny dried fish resembling white bait provided much of our protein source. We kept some chickens, which gave us a few eggs occasionally. We also grew our own vegetables. I became quite proficient in cultivating sweet corn. Every day, I would go out to the surrounding fields and collect dung left by grazing cattle. This makes excellent fertiliser.

My sisters, who were one and two years older than me had their hair cut very short to disguise them as boys to avert potential assault. In the house where we lived, there was a cellar with a trapdoor hidden beneath floorboards where my parents concealed us whenever Japanese soldiers were seen approaching the house.

Our family was fortunate to survive intact over the five years of Japanese rule. The Americans finally ended the war in Asia by dropping nuclear bombs on Hiroshima and Nagasaki. Leaving aside the question whether this is morally justifiable, we, the people of South-East Asia, will always be grateful to be rescued from the tyranny of occupation. Following Japan's surrender, Malaya was 'liberated' by British forces in September 1945.

But peace was short lived. War against the Japanese was followed by hostilities with the communists. The defeat by the Japanese heralded the end of the British Empire. The brown man has prevailed over the white man. Many people felt this was a cause for celebration. Nationalistic calls for independence resounded in the colonies. In Malaya, the Malayan Communist Party (MCP) wanted to form a communist government and set out to disrupt the country. In June 1948, a state of emergency was declared in Malaya after the murder of three European rubber planters. The most notorious event was the assassination of the British High Commissioner, Sir Henry Gurney in an ambush on a quiet road outside the capital on 6 October 1951. The place where it happened was at the 56½th mile of Kuala Kubu Road that leads up to Fraser's Hill, a popular hill station resort. A sign there now marks the spot. The road snakes through dense tropical forest, providing perfect concealment for the assailants. Today, this area is still rather eerie. I have driven along it many times.

Malaya gained her independence on 31 August 1957 and became Malaysia after incorporating the states of Sarawak and Sabah in Borneo. Even after independence, armed conflict between the MCP and Malaysian federal security forces continued. This ended on 2 December 1989, when the MCP agreed to a ceasefire and was dissolved. The conflict lasted 21 years, 5 months, 2 weeks and 1 day. Without the help of British and Commonwealth troops, Malaysia could have become a communist state. This is a fine chapter in Britain's colonial history.

I missed most of this tumultuous period as I was away in Britain for my studies.

During the Japanese occupation, our large family house was used as headquarters by the high command. The rumour was that many atrocities were committed there and even beheadings were carried out on the premises. We couldn't possibly return to the house with that kind of history. We sold it after the war. That was the first significant break from the past. The house is now a shopping mall and a bowling alley.

There was another reason to why we moved. It held memories of a sad family event which happened before the war. I had a younger brother who died there in 1936. He was just one year old. He had leukaemia. I remember vaguely the gloom that descended on the house but I was too young to fully understand the depth of my parents' grief. After the war, our family moved to Penang, my mother's hometown.

3. Tropical Childhood

In the 16th century, the Malacca Strait, a stretch of water between the Malay Peninsula and the Indonesian island of Sumatra, was at the centre of the global spice trade, linking the Indian Ocean and the Pacific Ocean. It is still one of the most important shipping lanes in the world.

Pulau Pinang (island of betel nut) lies at the northern entrance of the Malacca Strait, just off the west coast of Malaysia. With its white sandy beaches fringed by swaying palm trees and tall casuarinas and washed over by the warm waters of the Andaman Sea, the island deserves its accolade as 'Pearl of the Orient'.

In 2008, Penang's George Town became a UNESCO Historic Site. The city is regarded as an exceptional example of a multicultural heritage with Malay, Chinese, Indian and European influence that is unique in South-East Asia.

At the centre of the city with a prime sea frontage stands the Eastern & Oriental Hotel (usually just referred to as the E&O). Founded in 1885 by two of the Armenian Sarkies brothers, it was once considered to be 'the Premier Hotel East of Suez'. Illustrious guests who had stayed there included Noel Coward, Somerset Maugham, Rudyard Kipling, Charlie Chaplin and many others.

I recommend anyone passing through Malaysia to visit Penang. Stay awhile in the E&O. At sundown, take a drink out onto the hotel's veranda, gaze across the sea and go back in time.

If you want to get a panoramic view of the whole island, go up to Penang Hill, the oldest hill station[1] in South-East Asia, dating back to the 18th century. At 800 m and thickly forested, the temperature is usually about 5 degrees cooler than in town, a pleasant respite from the heat and humidity down below. Today, it is a popular venue for both locals and visitors.

---

1 A hill station typically refers to a town or settlement located at a higher elevation than the nearby plain or valley areas. Hill stations are known for their cooler climates, scenic beauty, and often offer breathtaking panoramic views of the surrounding landscapes. Many hill stations are established by colonial powers in the past, primarily as summer resorts to escape the scorching heat of the lowlands.

Penang Hill is accessible by a funicular railway which opened in 1923. As the train climbs slowly upwards, take note of the subtle changes in the vegetation. Ferns and orchids begin to appear on the hillside. My favourite are monkey cups, the carnivorous tropical pitcher plants. They are called monkey cups because monkeys are said to drink the fluid collected inside the pitchers. Insects are attracted by the scent of nectar. They fall into the fluid and are digested by enzymes, providing nutrients for the plants. I am fascinated by this gruesome botanical example of the interplay between prey and predator.

It is possible to walk up Penang Hill. There is a rugged 3-mile trail to the top which takes about 4 hours to complete. It is described as 'challenging', being uphill all the way. This route is usually regarded as an adventurous experience rather than an alternative to the funicular railway. I have done it once with the boy scouts at school. On that occasion, we were joined by the girl guides from the convent, making it altogether a delightful day out.

Apart from a brief period during the Japanese occupation when we had to learn Japanese, all my education was in the English medium. This has been the family tradition ever since Grandfather came to Malaya. He was far-sighted enough to see the importance of English as a means of communication and was one of the first to have English-educated employees, including Europeans, on his staff.

I went to a tiny village school called St Xavier's, run by Catholic Brothers, a legacy of past missionary activity in Penang. The school was chosen because it was conveniently located just next door to where we lived, so I could walk there and back.

Unusual for such a humble academic institution, the school, surprisingly, offered Latin in its curriculum. This proved to be a valuable asset when I went to boarding school in England. Ironically, Latin is now fast disappearing from schools in Britain and the government is trying to revive it.

School only functioned in the morning. There were no afternoon sessions and, mercifully, very little homework. So, for the rest of the afternoon, I was left to my own devices.

I bred chickens and ducks, their young following me every-

Latin class of St. Xavier's in 1947

where like the geese bonding with ethologist Konrad Lorenz. I would take my charges to forage in the orchard of rambutan trees behind our house. Once, a duckling came too close to my spade as I was digging for worms for them and I accidentally fractured one of its legs. I tried my best to bandage it with a splint. Unfortunately, my surgical skill wasn't up to it and the duckling died the next day. Maybe this was for the best, but I was distraught.

I also had a pet mongoose to protect me from snakes—and there were many poisonous ones around. King cobras were often seen slithering along the floor of our garage as I collected my bicycle in the morning. We were also told to shake our shoes or slippers before putting them on in case poisonous scorpions were lurking within. These are part and parcel of life in the tropics.

I once tried to set up a saltwater aquarium. With the sea all around me, I thought this should be easy to do. But it was not a success. Creating an artificial marine environment was more difficult than expected. I had to settle on the usual freshwater model. Many varieties of exotic tropical fishes were available. One of the most beautiful is the brilliantly coloured Siamese fighting fish, with its elaborate fins and tails, the aquatic equivalent of the peacock's flamboyant display. But only a single fish of this species can be placed in one aquarium. More than one will fight continuously.

Living on an island, the sea, of course, played a large part in our activities. We could all swim but we never had proper swimming lessons on how to do the freestyle, breaststroke, etc. We learnt to swim as a by-product of other activities, such as waterskiing. When I arrived at boarding school in England, there was some excitement that here was a boy from a tropical island who might be a useful member of the swimming team. I was a big disappointment.

Like a tropical Huckleberry Finn, I spent many happy hours along the shore or sitting on the sea wall casting my home-made fishing rod into the waves with more hope than expectation for a catch. The very occasional success was enough to justify the hours spent. Time seemed infinite.

I learnt from local fishermen how to capture worms for bait. Chew some bread; wait for a wave to recede; spit on the wet sand and worms would pop up to the surface; grab hold of the head and gently pull it up. Voila, bait for the fish hook. Easier said than done. Unless one is extremely quick, the worm would disappear back into its hole. I spent more time catching bait than actually fishing. But it was all part of the ritual.

View from Penang House

Low tide was the time to dig for *siput*, tiny clams that are delicious. An hour or so of digging would produce enough to take home for the cook to make into a tasty dish, a kind of Oriental vongole with chilli and soya sauce.

On the subject of food, the Peranakan cuisine is a unique blend of Chinese, Malay and Indian influence with a sprinkling of Thai from across the border, that is found nowhere else outside Penang.

Among my favourites is *asam laksa*, noodles in a spicy, sweet and sour fish base soup. *Asam* means 'tamarind' which gives the stock its distinctive sour flavour. Outside Penang, there are other types of laksa, mostly in a coconut base curry sauce or *lemak*. Assam is an acquired taste. Some people might find it too sharp.

Char kuey teow is another favourite. In Hokkien, *char* means 'stir-fried' and *kuey teow* is flat rice noodles. The basic ingredients usually include chilli, eggs and clams. I once took my youngest daughter, Imogen, to sample this dish. She is allergic to eggs, cannot tolerate hot chillies and is wary of eating clams. When I requested the cook to leave out these items for her, he groaned, 'I have nothing left to fry except noodles!'

For dessert, I will go straight for *pulut tai tai*. The story goes that this was once made for the wives (*tai tai*) of rich merchants. It is Penang *nyonya*'s classic pudding—a pressed glutinous rice cake steamed in coconut milk and eaten together with creamy coconut *kaya* jam. The *pulut* (glutinous rice) is stained its characteristic blue colour by pigment extracted from the butterfly pea flower.

This will be followed by *kuih talam*, a steamed green colour pandan cake topped with a canopy of white coconut cream, giving it the signature 2-colour scheme. In Malay, *kuih* means 'cake' and *talam* is 'tray' because the cake is set in a mould.

Finally, to round up a meal, there is *chendol* which my children call 'green worms'. These are noodles dyed green with juice from pandan leaves, served in a bowl of coconut milk with shaved ice and a topping of syrup of gula malacca.

Eating all this leisurely al fresco at a hawker's stall by the sea is an experience to savour. As I write this, my taste buds are tingling. Ask Penangites living abroad what they miss most from home and they will say, food.

I had never paid much attention to the origins of the Penang cuisine until now when I started writing about it. There is so much overlap between Malay and Straits Chinese culture.

I learnt to play tennis in Penang and became quite proficient in the sport. I didn't realise then what an asset this would be at boarding school in England (see Chapter 4). It was unusual for boys of my age to play tennis which was considered rather 'posh'. Most would go for badminton which was, and still is, Malaysia's national sport.

Some of my friends had their own tennis courts so there was no shortage of venues for practice. They lived in grand colonial-style mansions in what was then called Northam Road, once dubbed 'the Millionaires' Row'. I would cycle to these lovely houses with a tennis racket in one hand and an ice cream cone in the other, precariously steering the bicycle. In those days, traffic was light and the roads, shaded by stately Angsana trees, were relatively empty of cars.

We had a good local tennis coach. He was reputed to have played at Wimbledon partnering my cousin in the mixed doubles. We did not have formal lessons as such. They were more like informal advice during genteel evening tennis parties in these big houses. But we managed to imbibe the fundamentals of the serve and volley, forehand and backhand. The ubiquitous double-handed backhand so common today wasn't invented then. I still think that the single-handed backhand as used by stars like Roger Federer is the more graceful stroke.

Many of these grand houses are still there. Some have been converted for commercial use but a few remain in private hands. We still have a few friends in Penang who continue to live in their mansions. We meet up whenever I visit Penang and reminisce about our carefree childhood days. Unlike me, they have never left the island. We have chosen different paths but a shared history kept our friendships alive. I sometimes wonder what life would have been like for me if I had stayed in Penang. There is a university in Penang. At one time, I did consider basing myself there.

We still have our own house which is further up the coast. Our garden used to sweep down to the sea. Across on the mainland,

Kedah Peak, one of the highest mountains in Malaysia, rises majestically from the surrounding paddy fields. From my bedroom, I could hear the gentle lapping of the waves. This was the soothing sound I missed when trying to get to sleep in the eerie silence of the dormitory at boarding school in Cambridge.

A constant breeze blew in from the sea. There was no air-conditioning then. We slept under mosquito nets with windows wide open. Nowadays, everyone is shut in air-conditioned rooms completely cut off from the distinctive sounds and smell of a tropical night. When the older generation claims that they had it better, the remark is usually treated as some kind of nostalgic prolapse. But in this case, I think we did have it better. At dawn, with the dew still fresh on the ground, is the best time of day in the tropics.

I used to sit on the balcony of our house looking out for a ship of the Blue Funnel Line to come into harbour. It usually carried a consignment of my favourite comic books. I knew these would be in the shops the next day after the ship's arrival. I would then cycle into town with much anticipation to collect them. My literary taste wasn't too sophisticated. I followed the adventures of Sheena, Queen of the Jungle!

These comic books usually included an advertisement from Charles Atlas, the bodybuilder, showing a bully kicking sand into the face of a skinny man on a beach. The message was, you don't have to suffer such indignity if you have a brawny physique. All you have to do is to buy a contraption called a 'Bullworker', a shining metal tube which you press together from both ends. In time, 'you too can have a body like mine', claimed Atlas.

As a rather puny youngster, I promptly bought one. But the result was disappointing. There was no discernible expansion of my biceps, nor of any other muscles for that matter. Today, I remain a puny adult.

The Bullworker is now downstairs in the basement of our house in Cambridge, together with other memorabilia from the past like my violin and skis. Each item has its own story to tell.

Our Penang house is now separated from the sea by a four-lane coastal highway called Gurney Drive. Worse is to come. The government plans to build a theme park on reclaimed land on the other side of the highway. Furthermore, all the buildings surrounding our house have been demolished, including my old school St Xavier's, and replaced by high-rise condominiums. Now, when I visit Penang, I have to search very hard to locate our house, dwarfed by these huge futuristic developments. It is a listed building. We are not allowed to alter it in any way. Nor do we want to, as it is a vital piece of our family history.

We have packed up the rosewood furniture inlaid with mother-of-pearl, our collection of multicoloured Straits Chinese porcelain and watercolours of Penang street scenes by artist Tan Choon Ghee. These are now in our house in Cambridge. They will help me recapture a vanished past.

I see my childhood days in Penang as the last real link I had with the tropics. They were happy times. From its shores in 1949, I sailed to austere post-war Britain. The excitement of travelling

Penang House

to a new country was tempered by a tinge of anxiety. What will life at boarding school be like?

Many of my favourite novels are about remembered childhood in the tropics. Arundhati Roy drew on her memories of growing up in Kerala as a background for her Booker Prize-winning novel

Furniture from the Penang House

The God of Small Things. So has Romesh Gunesekera in *Suncatcher*, about two friends growing up in Ceylon before it became Sri Lanka. I like these stories because they are images of my own life in different settings.

4. Boarding School

As children of the colonies, many Malaysians go to Britain for further studies, usually for university, but some, like me, are sent off to boarding school at an earlier age. Whenever I returned home during school holidays, I was usually greeted by, 'Are you back from overseas?'

The advantages and disadvantages of sending young children away from their own family environment to be looked after by some impersonal institution have long been a topic of debate. Those in favour claim that the child will develop a sense of independence while those against accuse the parents of harmful neglect which will have grave emotional consequences for the child.

The school environment was certainly very different from the one at home in Malaysia. As the only son and heir, I was the centre of attention and, some might say, rather spoilt. At boarding school, I was just one boy among many others and thus treated the same way. The feeling that I was nothing special after all got rid of my conceited sense of entitlement. I also learnt to be self-reliant without servants always at my beck and call. Overall, I think boarding school away from the indulgent ambience of home was good for me. I don't remember ever feeling homesick.

In the summer before starting school, our parents took us on a grand tour of Europe, exploring the cities and coastlines of Switzerland, France and Italy. I found Geneva, Nice, Monte Carlo, St-Tropez, Rome, Florence, Venice and Capri most memorable. It was a whirlwind introduction to another world, one that is so grand and sophisticated.

I was a boarder at the Leys School in Cambridge from 1949 until 1953. It is a minor public school, but, because it is located in Cambridge, it is relatively well-known and has a good reputation. Since my time there, many more Malaysians have passed through the school. I believe there is now a flourishing old boys' association in Malaysia.

One famous old boy was James Hilton, the author of *Good-bye, Mr. Chips,* published in 1934. It is a touching story about a beloved housemaster who spent his whole life teaching at a fictitious boys' boarding school called Brookfield (based on the Leys School). His life was unremarkable and left only a faint footprint but he was fulfilled. Mr Chips lodged in a house at Brookside just across the road from the school. That row of terrace houses still stands.

The book was made into a film. There were three versions. The first, in black and white, starred Robert Donat, the second was with Peter O'Toole and the third with Martin Clunes. These attest to the wide appeal of the novel over many generations.

My daughter Tracey gave me a 1st edition of *Good-bye, Mr. Chips* signed by the author as a birthday present many years ago. This volume now stands proudly in the centre of the bookcase in my study at home. Every now and then I would remove it carefully from the shelf and re-read the entire story to get a picture of what school days must have been like at the Leys for the generations before me.

Hilton also wrote *Lost Horizon*, a story featuring a faraway enchanted monastery in the high mountains of Tibet which he named 'Shangri-La'. Ever since then, the name has become synonymous with any utopian destination.

A more contemporary figure is J.G. Ballard, whose novel *Empire of the Sun* was turned into a film by Steven Spielberg. The book recalls Ballard's childhood experience in a Japanese prison camp in Shanghai during the Second World War. The book was published in 1984. It took him almost 40 years to make up his mind to write it. We both suffered under Japanese rule but in two different countries.

Ballard was just a few years older than me. He also went up to King's College, Cambridge after the Leys but had left both these places before I arrived. I never got to know him.

Many people detest their boarding school days, describing the period as 'hellish'. I didn't mind my time at the Leys, although it wasn't all that memorable. It certainly wasn't like *Tom Brown's School Days*, the 1857 novel by Thomas Hughes. Modern day public schools are now more civilised. No more flogging, at least not at the Leys! I rather liked the regimented lifestyle where every minute of the day was scheduled for a particular activity. It removed the day-to-day decision making. It is like ordering a 'tasting menu' in a restaurant where the chef selects all the dishes. One does not have to waste time and energy wading through the extensive menu. Just sit back and go with the flow.

I was never bullied at school. Perhaps being good at games saved me. As I described earlier (see Chapter 3), I played a lot of tennis in my early years in Penang and was already quite proficient at the sport. When I arrived at the Leys, I was immediately selected to play in the school's 1st tennis team in the following summer term. This was unusual, to have a new boy in his first year play in the school's first team in any sport. I eventually became captain of tennis. In a boys' school, to be

The first tennis team at the Leys School

good at sports is a distinct advantage. It eased my entry into what was, for me, an alien environment and into being accepted by my fellow pupils.

I blended in comfortably at school but the outside world was different. One year, the school took a team to the Easter hockey festival in Hanover, Germany. Each boy was to stay with a German family. When our train arrived at Hanover, our German hosts were waiting to welcome us at the station. All the other boys were quickly snapped up but nobody came for me. Finally, a boy about my own age came up, took me by the hand and said: 'You come with me.' I was so relieved to be rescued that I can still remember his aristocratic-sounding name: Dieter von Frankenberg.

At the time, I didn't pay too much attention to the incident. But on reflection, I wonder if this was my first experience of racial discrimination. I was the only brown boy in the team.

There was no corporal punishment at school. Misdemeanours were punished simply by writing the school lines: 'Few things are more distressing to a well-regulated mind than to see a boy disporting himself at improper moments.' The number of lines to be written depended on the severity of the offence. An essential element of the punishment was the lines had to be done in class during 'break', when everyone else was out and about enjoying their free time. The more lines to be written, the longer it would take to complete and the more free time was lost.

I have written these lines so often that, now 70 years later, I can still quote them from memory! My crime, if you can call it a crime, was usually being late for breakfast. Every morning, the school bell would ring for assembly in the dining hall for breakfast. When the bell stopped, each boy had to be standing by his place at the table fully dressed. I found it impossible to knot my tie properly while running from dormitory to the dining hall. I once tried to cheat by buying a clip-on tie to use specifically for the morning run. But it was discovered by Matron and confiscated.

There were other quaint rules that had to be observed. One such was, only prefects were allowed to put their hands in their trouser pockets. Who would come up with such a bizarre idea?

The benefit of boarding school is that every hour of the day is usefully employed. There was plenty of time for extracurricular activities such as music. I sang in the chapel choir and in the chorus of Gilbert and Sullivan's *Mikado* and *The Pirates of Penzance*.

I became a lifelong fan of these composers and have a collection of all their operettas. There were also jolly evenings singing madrigals, an activity considered rather sissy by the more macho members of the school.

I played the violin in the school orchestra. A fleeting moment of fame was a solo performance at the school annual concert. I wanted to play Toselli's *Serenade* but the music master disdainfully dismissed the piece as being more suitable for the palm-court foyer of some posh hotel. Then there was *Le Cygne* (The Swan) by Saint-Saëns but this piece was deemed to be more suitable for cello than violin. We eventually settled on Gounod's *Ave Maria*. This turned out to be a discerning choice. It is a charming melodic piece that ends with the final note of the violin quietly fading away while the piano accompaniment lingers on for a few more bars. Even now, this beautiful closing passage never fails to move me every time I hear it.

A BBC radio programme called *Desert Island Discs* invites guests to make a list of musical scores they would take with them if they became marooned on a desert island and the reason for their choice. Not that I will ever be invited but for me, Gounod's *Ave Maria* would certainly be one of them because my mind goes back to that evening in the school hall, where I tried my best to make good music.

After leaving school, I never played the violin again. Maybe I was intimidated by the very high standards of the musicians at university. Everyone seemed to be a member of the National Youth Orchestra. I felt inadequate in the midst of such brilliance. The transition from school to university can be a chastening experience. I still have my violin. It is presently in the cellar. I have often thought of taking it up again but never got round to doing it.

One of my favourite musical pieces is Isaac Stern playing Brahms's Violin Concerto in D major. Another is Bizet's *Pearl Fishers* sung by Jussi Björling and Robert Merrill. I have heard many other duets but this is the only one that makes me cry. I still have the original vinyl records together with many others. These are now coming back into fashion. I haven't replaced them with their CD reincarnations.

I used to be a high-fidelity audio enthusiast and had built up a stereo system comprising a Thorens turntable, a Quad II amplifier and a pair of Wharfedale speakers, all of which were considered to be top of the range at that time. I bought these in the early 1950s from outlets at London's Tottenham Court Road which was then the mecca for hi-fi equipment. They are still with me but have not been used for a very long time. I am now in the process of rejuvenating the system.

Biology was my favourite subject. Dissecting a dogfish, looking at the inside of an earthworm or examining the intricate patterns of a flower in the practical class was fascinating. I found chemistry boring and physics impenetrable. These were the subjects I had to take to read medicine in Cambridge.

I remember the physics practical exam. It was a disaster. We had to find the specific gravity (SG) of an unknown solution using a capillary tube with a specified diameter. This should be a simple procedure. Stick the capillary into the solution and measure how high the solution rises within the tube. From this measurement together with the known diameter of the capillary, the SG of the solution can be determined from a formula.

When I did this, the solution did not rise. Panic! I subsequently discovered this was because a small piece of plasticine had become embedded inside the opening of one end of the capillary, blocking the entry of the solution.

In desperation, I tasted the solution. It had the saltiness of saline. I knew the SG of saline, so I worked backwards and made up the calculation. I should be commended for ingenuity and dedication. The unknown solution could have been cyanide!

I had the fanciful idea of becoming a marine biologist like Jacques Cousteau, the French oceanographer with his undersea world. It has an aura of romance, a dash of glamour and a hint of adventure. But in those days to become a doctor or a lawyer was the pinnacle of social and professional achievement. Anything else was considered to be frivolous activity. I was persuaded to become a doctor.

Greta Burkill

The person who guided me through my early school years was Greta Burkill, my Cambridge guardian. She was married to Charles Burkill, a Fellow of Peterhouse who later became Master of the College. I called them Mummy B and Daddy B.

Greta was passionate about education and was a well-known figure in the University. She played a big part in the founding of New Hall[2], the third women's college in Cambridge. My sister Ruby and I endowed a Greta Burkill Fellowship there to commemorate her.

Collegiate Cambridge has always looked after their Fellows

2 Today, this college is known as Murray Edwards College.

and undergraduates well. Little attention was paid to postgraduates. Greta became aware of this anomaly and was dismayed to find that they felt isolated. She created the Graduate Society, which today is housed at the University Graduate Centre, an imposing building overlooking the beautiful vista of the Mill Pond. It contains a variety of amenities, such as a food hall, a formal restaurant, a common room, etc. Thanks to Greta Burkill, the graduate community now has its own home.

Cambridge also provided scant hospitality for academics visiting from other universities. To rectify this deficiency, Greta founded the Society for Visiting Scholars. Almost single-handedly, she set up housing schemes, schools for accompanying children and a social life for wives.

Because of all her activities, Greta was a prominent and respected figure in the academic community. She knew everyone and everyone knew her. Greta's life is fully captured by Rosemary Pattenden in *Greta Burkill: Mother to Thousands*.

At the Leys School, all boys had to take a foreign language. As English is not my first language, Greta argued that I should be exempted from this extra burden.

'My boy, Wai, he is Chinese!' Greta confronted the surprised Headmaster when we met him in his office. Greta won the argument. I was allowed to skip the foreign language subject. I sometimes regret not having taken French, for this would have been useful for my subsequent travels in Europe.

I lived with the Burkills during most school holidays. For the first time, I experienced life without domestic servants. I made my own bed, vacuumed the floor, peeled vegetables, washed dishes after meals and much more! It was a steep learning curve. After dinner, everyone sat down to talk or read. There was no television—very much an academic household.

To supplement our meagre pocket money, Guy and I bred ferrets to sell in the Cambridge cattle market, where we established quite a lucrative trade. Through a great deal of painful trial and error, we learnt how to handle these ferocious creatures with their sharp teeth. It was worthwhile, for the financial return was good. School allowed us one shilling and sixpence per week, of which six pence were for a compulsory chapel donation.

It was Guy who first started calling me 'Charlie'. Through constant usage, everyone now knows me by this nickname so I have continued with it for ease of communication. I realise that part of my identity has been effaced. For official documents and scientific papers, I retain my full Chinese name of Yung Wai (Y.W.), which can be translated as 'courageous and noble'. My parents had unrealistically high expectations! Guy qualified as a chemical engineer. He worked for the oil company Shell and spent most of his life in the jungle of South America. 'He has gone native' was how Greta described him. I never saw Guy again after we left Cambridge.

On the morning of my last day at school, I took a walk quietly around the tennis courts where I had spent so many happy hours. I thought about the range of emotions I had experienced, from elation when I won the school tennis championship to despair when I was dropped from the first team in disgrace for unsporting behaviour. I was seen banging my racquet on top of the net in frustration. This seems a trivial infringement compared to what we now see coming from professional players. But in school, this was an unacceptable offence.

From school, I went up to King's College, Cambridge and then onwards to clinical training at St Thomas' Hospital in London.

5. King's College

I arrived at King's College, Cambridge, as an undergraduate in 1953. My uncle, Loke Wan Tho (see Chapter 2), was also there in 1933, reading English. Two generations of Lokes have been alumni of King's.

The College published a book in 1980 entitled *Kingsmen of a Century* by Patrick Wilkinson. Almost an entire page is devoted to Wan Tho, who built up a vast business empire in Singapore. Tagged on at the end of his biography are four short sentences mentioning that I, his nephew, had become a Fellow of the College. I felt somewhat short-changed! I had thought that gaining a College Fellowship deserved a bit more recognition. Still, I mustn't complain. At least I made an entry, brief though it is.

My academic record wasn't that brilliant but I managed to pass all the necessary exams that enabled me to move into my clinical studies in London. In those far-off days, life was not as competitive as it is now.

I did not approach my university education as a stepping stone to a career or employment. It was simply a rite of passage. Had I known then that I was heading towards a career in academia, I probably would have tried harder. As the comedian Spike Milligan once said, 'If I had known I would live for so long, I would have taken better care of myself.' Fortunately, I managed to salvage some intellectual credibility later.

Following my undistinguished performance in the first year Tripos examination, I received a curt note from my Director of Studies, warning me that, unless I applied myself more diligently to my studies, he would have to transfer me from Medical Sciences to an easier option, such as Land Economy. That was my wake-up call. I still have that letter among my other memorabilia.

One evening, I was telling this story to a few colleagues at dinner in College. A guest was sitting nearby who overheard our conversation. As luck would have it, he happened to be a land economist. 'The subject is now much more rigorous,' he said. Oops!

Graduation with BA in 1956

In Cambridge in the 1950s, time passed at a gentle pace. Lectures and practical classes in the mornings and supervisions in the evenings. Sports in the afternoon (I was captain of tennis and also played hockey for College) or just lazy days punting on the river; toasted crumpets for tea; playing bridge accompanied by sherry after dinner. Occasionally, we did some revision. The long vacation term in summer was the favourite period. Most other undergraduates would leave town. Only medical students stayed. We had to attend a course in pharmacology which was not too onerous.

I was allotted a room on A staircase in College, directly opposite the set occupied by E.M. Forster. I was very excited to have such a famous literary figure as a neighbour. As someone who grew up under British rule, I can relate to the characters portrayed in Forster's *A Passage to India*, set against the backdrop of the Raj.

The bathroom for A staircase at that time was located in another courtyard around the corner. One morning, as I was walking there in my dressing gown with my toiletries, a group of American tourists looked at me with astonishment. I overheard one saying to another, 'I didn't know these ruins are inhabited!'

Undergraduates were not permitted to have pets but the rules were unclear about caged birds. I kept a Roseate cockatoo called Corky in my college room. Corky was sufficiently tame to be let out of the cage when I was present. Unfortunately, it had the destructive habit of chewing up my lecture notes, a novel twist to 'the dog ate my homework'!

One potentially disastrous incident stands out in my memory. I was driving with a fellow King's student to the seaside in Norfolk when we had a horrific crash because I entered a corner too fast. According to the police investigation afterwards, we snapped off one of those tall wooden telegraph poles and threw the upper portion 88 feet away. The impact must have been massive. I can still recall that moment with total clarity. I could see we were heading relentlessly towards the telegraph pole but the car seemed to have a will of its own. It was like those surreal nightmares where one has no control of events. We didn't have seat belts in those days. Miraculously, we both survived but landed in hospital. My passenger had a gash in the neck. Another centimetre either way, the carotid artery would be severed with fatal consequence.

I thought I would definitely be sent down from the University. I had committed three cardinal sins. First, I did not have a permit for my car. Undergraduates were not allowed to own a car unless they had special needs. Second, I did not have an exeat to travel beyond the ten-mile radius of Cambridge during full term. Finally, I almost killed a fellow undergraduate by dangerous driving.

Fortunately, I was spared this ultimate sanction but was warned that there must not be a repeat of such an incident. I will never forget this episode. Today, I drive very carefully, although I am still very much into sports cars.

Patrick Wilkinson was Senior Tutor at the time of the accident. He held my fate in his hands. He happened to be a contemporary of uncle Wan Tho at King's. During their undergraduate days, he was a passenger in Uncle's Mercedes when they too survived a serious accident. Perhaps this experience made him treat me more leniently.

I came across an interesting article entitled 'Loke's Merc' by the well-known travel writer Norman Lewis (*Independent Magazinee*, 24 December 1988). He tells how he met Wan Tho and his Mercedes just by chance in 1937. They struck up a curious friendship as both men were car enthusiasts.

Norman Lewis was reminded of this encounter which occurred more than fifty years ago when an article appeared in a national newspaper in August 1988 about a 1936 Mercedes Grand Tourer that was sold for the exorbitant sum of £1,585,000. This extraordinary price was because the car was right-hand drive, being only one of two such models built out of a total production of 356. Wan Tho's 500K model was also right-hand drive. Was this the same car being auctioned? I tried to find out what happened to Uncle's Mercedes but no-one has any recollection.

I am a bit envious that, while Uncle had such an exquisite Mercedes in his undergraduate days, I made do with a humble Ford Prefect which couldn't hold a corner at speed. Ah well. Different times. Different lives.

Going through my student files recently, I found that Norman Lewis's daughter, Samara, was one of my medical students at King's. I was her Director of Studies. I had no idea then that her father had known my uncle in the 1930s. It is curious how our lives are interconnected in one way or another if we look back far enough.

After my accident, no motor insurance company would take me on for my next car. My profile and history would scare off all but the bravest agent.

History: Previous car write-off.
Present car: Triumph TR2 sports convertible.
Colour: Red.
Occupation: Medical student.
Age: 21

Somehow, I found a company that was willing to give me a quote. The company was Howe and Company, run by a Mr Howe. We became good friends. Today, 70 years later, his company still insures my cars. Mr Howe has long passed away but his company lives on. They deserve my loyalty.

In 1973, exactly twenty years from the time I came up as an undergraduate, I became a Fellow of King's. I had crossed the dividing line from being just an alumnus of the College to a Member of the Governing Body.

The letter, dated 8 June 1973, came in the morning post informing me that the College Council has elected me as a College Lecturer in Pathology and Director of Studies in Medical Sciences, to succeed Professor Kendal Dixon who was about to retire. It is impossible to put into words how I felt at the moment I opened the letter. How does one react when a dream becomes reality? I read it again and again to make sure I hadn't misinterpreted the message. I remember cycling furiously from our house to the village where Penny was shopping to tell her the good news. My election was officially announced locally in the *Cambridge Evening News* and nationally in *The Times* on Thursday, 26 July 1973.

In Cambridge, you do not apply to be a Fellow of a college. You wait to be invited. To be welcomed back by my own college is especially gratifying. King's is one of the most prestigious colleges in Cambridge. Gaining a Fellowship there is a much coveted glittering prize.

I was lucky to be in the right place at the right time. I fulfilled a teaching need in College following Kendal's retirement. We taught the same subject and were attached to the same University Department, so it was a seamless transition. There was no official interview. Members of Council invited me for lunch one day, presumably to 'look me over' to see if I would 'fit in'. All very low key and civilised. Most importantly, I must have received the support of Kendal himself. If I have to single out one person who had the greatest impact on my professional life, it must be Kendal

Professor Kendal Dixon (right) and Professor Ronald Greaves (Head of Department of Pathology)

Dixon. In the Prologue, I mentioned that he gave me the idea of applying for the position in the Department of Pathology which started my academic career.

Sadly, Kendal developed Alzheimer's in his later years and was essentially lost to us long before he died on 17 December 1990 aged 79. He was a kind, gentle and cultured man. Penny used to go to their house and sit with Kendal while Ann Dixon went shopping. And I used to take Kendal to dine in College so he had a chance to get out of the house. On one occasion, halfway through dinner, Kendal suddenly stood up and said in a loud voice, 'Charlie, I want to go home.' All conversation stopped. But nobody was embarrassed by the interruption. People just smiled knowingly while we walked out from High Table. Normally, one is not allowed to leave until dinner is formally ended and Grace is said.

At the 1996 College Annual Congregation, someone raised the question whether the Fellowship at King's is too heavily weighted towards graduates of the College. This prompted Dr George Salt, a senior Fellow, to do a survey. These are his findings: of the Provost and 109 Fellows in 1996, 30 had been undergraduates at King's, 17 were at other colleges in Cambridge, 21 did their undergraduate work at Oxford and the rest were from other universities. While Oxbridge provided a large number of our Fellows, King's itself was not over-represented.

It was different in the past. The change in composition of the Fellowship came about around the 1960s. Those elected before that date mostly did their undergraduate and postgraduate work at King's, but of those elected since 1960, a much smaller proportion were King's alumni. Back in 1936, things were very different. Of the 46 Fellows, 40 were King's undergraduates. There is, therefore, a distinct shift in diversity of the academic sources of the Fellowship over the years. This information should be of interest to sociologists.

On the subject of diversity, College once held a party in Hall for children of Fellows. Hall is adorned with portraits of past Fellows from bygone eras. In one of the games, children were asked to run around and stand beneath 'the one that looked most like Daddy'. Of course, for my children, there was no portrait that remotely resembled Daddy! They were awarded consolation prizes as the game was deemed to be unfair.

College recently commissioned the artist Anna Paik to paint my portrait. I have sat for her on several occasions. She suggested I wear my scarlet doctoral gown over a Chinese costume. These will represent my dual Asian heritage and academic career.

The background will be my room in King's against a window with views across to the river or King's Chapel. The portrait was unveiled at a ceremony on 23 September 2023.

Where will it hang? It really doesn't matter. I am just immensely proud as the first Asian Fellow in the 800-year history of King's to be honoured in this way. Maybe, if another children's party were to be held in College again, there will be a portrait that 'looks like Daddy'.

Kendal was Director of Studies for Medical Sciences at King's 1958–1973, when I replaced him. I myself retired in 2002. Between us, we have occupied that position for 44 years. Kendal

My portrait, painted by Anna Paik

was very proud of his Fellowship at King's as I am. He was a warm and hospitable mentor to all the undergraduates under his care. I try to follow his example and treat my own students in the same way.

Being a Director of Studies (DoS) is a full-time job. It is both academic and pastoral. We cannot separate the two. Students' personal troubles will affect their academic performance. I have spent many hours (and used up many boxes of tissues) comforting tearful students who come to see me with what appears to them to be implacable problems. This happens especially frequently at exam times. On some occasions, I've even had to drag a reluctant student to the examination hall who was too panic-stricken to go.

Once, a student came to see me very disappointed with his Tripos exam results: 'In school, I was always top of the class but now I am not even average.' In the highly competitive world outside school, the top dog is reduced to a lowly member of the pack. This is the harsh lesson they all had to learn.

As DoS, my job was to organise college teaching for King's students in all the relevant Tripos subjects. As College Lecturer, I myself supervised them in Pathology, a subject that Kendal used to teach. The college supervision system, called the 'tutorial system' in Oxford, is unique to Oxbridge. This is when a small group of students (usually no more than 3 or 4) meets up with their supervisor to discuss a subject in greater depth than what is presented in their formal departmental lectures.

It is also an occasion for the supervisor to pick out those students who might be lagging behind and to monitor their progress closely. In small group teaching, there is nowhere for an ill-prepared student to hide.

In a recent letter to *The Times*, a student lamented that a residual hangover is indeed difficult to disguise during a supervision. A supervisor (from King's) followed with a letter the next day that this is not the sole prerogative of the student!

Some students remember their supervisions years or even decades later. Here is an email which I received dated 2 March 2021.

> Dear Charlie (if I may?),
> There is no reason that you should remember me but you supervised me in Pathology IB (Natural Sciences) in

1974–75 at King's. Not only did you make the subject very interesting, but you did me a great service in criticising my dreadful essay writing. I'm not sure that I would describe myself as a good writer even today, but you certainly made me take much more care.
Please accept my belated thanks!
Best wishes, David

He is now a Professor.

I often wore an ancient cardigan with gaping holes around the elbows during supervisions. The students were amused to see my decrepit attire. Just before Christmas one year, a parcel arrived in my room. It contained a brand new cardigan of exactly the same size and colour. They had clubbed together and bought it for me. I shall never forget this extraordinary generous gesture. I still have that cardigan which I keep in College to wear as an extra layer when the creaking heating system loses its battle with the winter cold outside. It is a gift I will always treasure.

In my own student days, I used to look forward to supervisions with Kendal Dixon. He had a huge store of eclectic anecdotes and quotations that made pathology come alive. Much to the envy of other King's students, Kendal often offered us sherry (always dry) after supervisions. Sometimes, this was replaced by a glass of wine. In addition to his many other college duties, Kendal was also the wine steward. I learnt a lot about the relative merits of different wines. Supervisions were held 6–7 in the evenings ending half an hour before dinner in Hall at 7.30. A preprandial drink was much appreciated by all.

Every year, we invited the medical students for lunch at home after the Tripos exams. Penny would spend days beforehand preparing the food. No matter how much food she cooked, it never seemed to be enough for their voracious appetites.

Our house is about 4 miles from the centre of Cambridge. The students arrived by a variety of transport: bicycle, car, taxi or bus. On one occasion, a girl student roared up to the house astride a huge motorcycle, clad in a biker's leather outfit which she peeled off to reveal a pretty summer frock underneath, like a butterfly emerging from its chrysalis. The day was spent sitting by the river which flows past our garden, walking in the neighbouring woodland or playing croquet on our bumpy moss-covered lawn. It was a relaxing day for them after the rigour of exams. Whenever I meet up with past students, this is an occasion they remember, even years afterwards.

Inviting the students into our own home for lunch instead of having it catered by College made the event more personal. The students themselves appreciated this. But Directors of Studies don't do this anymore. Nowadays, academics simply do not have the time to go this extra mile.

On graduation day, College entertains the students' parents in the Provost's garden. This is when, as DoS, I met the parents socially for the first time. Talking to them, I could sense their pride and joy at what their children had achieved. It was a joyful occasion. My parents never came for my own graduation. I can't even remember who was there.

When hoards of anxious-looking students suddenly appear in College, it is interview time. This period is just as stressful for the interviewer as it is for the interviewee. The outside world scrutinised our every move. There is this perception (false) that Oxbridge dons are out to fox unwary candidates with tricky questions. We had to be very careful what questions we asked and how we asked them.

I was caught out once. A candidate came with very impressive grades, full of As and A*s but fell down badly in the language, Urdu. 'Oh dear. What happened to Urdu?' I enquired gently, just to start our conversation. This was a mistake. The next day, an article appeared in a national newspaper accusing me of upsetting the candidate with an unfair question unrelated to medical sciences.

When interviews were over, it usually took me a few days to get back to my normal routine. I kept on thinking about those candidates we had rejected. We had sat in judgement and decided their fate. This was a heavy responsibility. What if we had made a mistake? It is usually quite easy to sort the best from the worst candidates but borderline cases are the ones who are difficult to evaluate. The number of applicants far exceeds the number we can accept. Medical Sciences is one subject with a strict quota imposed by the government.

In King's four Fellows took part in the interviews, working in pairs. Each candidate was seen for 30 minutes by one pair of the Fellows, followed by a further 30 minutes with another pair. At the end, we met up to compare notes and come to a collective decision. I think we had done all we could to be fair.

When I was an undergraduate, King's admitted four medical students per year. Today, we take in eight. This is still a relatively small number compared to other colleges. King's never had a medical tradition. Medicine, with its vocational leaning, was deemed not to be intellectually respectable. Natural sciences, mathematics and economics are the principal subjects. Even we, medical students, took the Natural Sciences Tripos examination. It was not until we reached clinical school that we became 'real' medics.

A college Fellowship is normally tied to a University post. But following my official retirement from the Department of Pathology, King's has generously re-elected me to a Life Fellowship, thus allowing me to continue with my academic life for as long as I wish. I am very fortunate not to experience the abrupt termination of a familiar lifestyle that usually accompanies retirement. I do not have to clear my desk immediately.

I still have my room (G3) in the Gibbs Building, one that I have occupied for over three decades. I often reflect on how privileged I am to be there, to gaze out onto the pristine back lawn sweeping down to the river Cam at the 'Backs' from one window and onto the iconic King's Chapel from another. This is where the BBC World Service broadcasts its annual Christmas Eve Carol Service on radio and television that has been performed for over 100 years.

At international conferences, it is customary for speakers to begin by showing a picture of where they work. When my turn comes round, I put up a photo of Gibbs Building next to the chapel taken from across the river, a familiar view that is featured on postcards and news bulletins about Cambridge. There is usually a murmur of appreciation when I point out the window of my room G3 and say, 'That is my office!' I am often tempted to press home my advantage even further and emulate Shelley's

Amanda and I, in front of the Chapel of King's and the Gibbs Building

Ozymandias: 'Look on my works, ye Mighty, and despair!'

But it is time for me to vacate my room and make way for the next generation of Fellows to move in. I have been slowly removing my personal effects that have accumulated over the years—to do a Marie Kondo clear-out.

The eclectic collection of books on the shelves opens a window into my life. Here are some examples: *The Porsche Handbook; Pathology of the Liver; Learn to Fly in a Tiger Moth; Diseases of Women; The English Country House; Human Implantation; How to Play Better Golf; Immunobiology of Trophoblast.* The contents of a bookshelf can reveal a great deal about the owner. I wonder what a stranger passing by would have made of me.

All these are now gone. I have erased my past. It is the end of an era.

The two new Fellows moving in are my former students. They have generously allowed me to continue to use G3 whenever I wish. Although the room is no longer 'mine', I will still have a base there for now.

King's is like a big multigenerational family. Most of the time, the relationship between members is harmonious. But it is not always so. I have two dear friends in College who refuse to speak to each other because of some disagreement in the past which still rankles. The philosopher Isaiah Berlin was once asked: 'Why are academic quarrels so bitter?' He replied: 'Because the stakes are so low.'

Each year, College publishes a list of Fellows according to age and seniority, with the oldest Fellow heading the list. I call this the 'Death List'. In 2021, I noted with alarm that I now occupy the top spot!

But, 'Age is an issue of mind over matter. If you don't mind, it doesn't matter,' wrote Mark Twain.

Nevertheless, it is a timely reminder. *Memento mori* ('remember you are mortal'), the slave whispered to Caesar as they made their triumphant return to Rome.

6. Clinical Years

From Cambridge, I moved on to St Thomas' Hospital in London (known affectionately by alumni as Tommy's) for my clinical studies.

This was an exciting time for medical students. At last, we encountered real patients. We could see we were almost at the end of our long journey to become doctors. Donning a white coat, with a stethoscope conspicuously displayed around our neck, we strutted through the hospital full of self-importance. In reality, we were just minor cogs in a large machine.

The comic novel *Doctor in the House* captures the life of clinical students perfectly. It was turned into a film starring Kenneth More and Dirk Bogarde. Richard Gordon, the author of the book, was himself a student at St Thomas'. My own experience there confirms that life indeed can be as hilarious as described by Gordon.

There was a time when it was considered rather 'cool' to have a relatively short tubing in our stethoscope. This was supposed to improve the acoustics. I had inadvertently cut mine just a little bit too short. During a ward round, while I was bending over to examine a patient, the consultant patted me on the back. 'You are meant to listen to his chest, not to smell him!' he whispered. Just as well it wasn't a female patient.

And there was the plantar reflex incident. In a healthy adult, when the sole of the foot is tickled with a blunt instrument, the big toe curves upwards. If it curves downwards, this signals some neurological disorder.

I could never get this reflex to work. Since it is likely to be normal in most patients, I usually just wrote in my notes: 'Plantar reflex normal in both feet.'

During a ward round, the consultant looked at my notes. 'That's interesting,' he said as he whipped back the bedclothes. The patient had one leg amputated below the knee!

Even my Final Exams had an episode worthy of inclusion in *Doctor in the House*. Candidates had what was called a 'Long Case', where they had to examine a patient with an undisclosed illness and make a diagnosis. When I asked the patient about his symptoms, he answered, 'I have lost my pain and temperature sensation but I have preserved my joint and position sense.' Wow! 'That sounds very complicated,' I murmured. I was totally thrown. I've never heard a patient describe his illness in this clinically precise way. Such specific symptoms should have given me a clue but I was so nervous I didn't make the connection.

The patient must have felt sorry for me. He beckoned me to come closer. 'I've got syringomyelia,' he whispered in my ear. This is a disease that affects the spinal column. He was one of those patients with a long-term illness who was constantly wheeled out for exam purposes and, over the years, had come to side with the students against their battle with the examiners. I felt it was a bit unfair for the examiners to use such a relatively unusual case but I won out in the end with the help of the patient. Honour was satisfied.

Final MB exams are relatively easy compared to Cambridge Tripos. The questions are more direct and straightforward. You either know the answer or you don't. They never include that dreaded word 'discuss' which frequently lurks at the end of Tripos questions. It might seem to be a harmless addition but ignore it at your peril. The difference between getting a Class 2.1 or 2.2 could depend on how well you 'discuss'. I passed. I was now a doctor with MB BChir after my name.

In those days, if you didn't pass the first time, you could try again and again indefinitely. *Doctor in the House* featured a character whose rich aunt left him a legacy with funds for him to use as long as he remained a medical student. He had no incentive to pass. There was a similar figure at Tommy's when I was there. I will not reveal his name as he came from a well-known aristocratic family. He was much older than the rest of us. We regarded him with awe and mistook him for a consultant.

But there were more serious moments. When learning midwifery, students had to accompany an obstetrician in a flying squad ambulance to deal with emergencies in a home delivery that had gone wrong. I shall never forget the scene in a case of post-partum haemorrhage where the whole bed was awash with blood. The human placenta, despite millions of years of evolution, is still not perfect. Many things can go wrong during pregnancy and at delivery when it refuses to detach from the womb.

I found midwifery rather daunting. One is responsible for two lives—mother and baby. And the human birth process is especially complicated. Delivering the baby requires skilled handling.

When humans started to walk on two legs about 6 million years ago, the shape of the pelvis changed dramatically. It became tilted and narrower. At the same time, the size of the baby's head in the womb has expanded due to the increasing size of the human brain. The combination of a narrow pelvis and a large baby's head means it is a tight fit with little room for manoeuvre.

Painful and powerful contractions are needed to push a baby out. No wonder the process is described as 'going into labour'. Human birth frequently needs a helping hand.

The compromise is for the human baby to be born before it gets too big, even if it is not fully developed. That is why the human offspring is so helpless when born.

One evening, I was in charge of taking notes at a difficult birth. The next day, during a ward round, we came to the bedside of the same woman.

'Whose patient is this?' barked the consultant. Silence. No-one answered.

After rummaging through the notes, he glared at me.

'Loke, she is your patient.'

'I am sorry, I didn't recognise her. I never saw her face!' I stammered.

St Thomas' Hospital still covers the area south of the River Thames where Somerset Maugham based his first novel *Liza of Lambeth* published in 1897. It is a tragic story of a miscarriage and domestic violence in the working-class district of Lambeth. Like Richard Gordon, Somerset Maugham was also a medical student at St Thomas'. The theme of their two novels cannot be more different. After the success of *Lisa of Lambeth*, Maugham gave up medicine in favour of literature.

As in my school and undergraduate days, sports continued to

be a major part of my life at Tommy's. There was, of course, tennis but my interest was already turning towards golf. I had a reasonable handicap of 10 at that time which was good enough to get me into the tail end of the hospital golf team.

London teaching hospitals have a long tradition of being associated with some of the famous golf clubs near London, such as Sunningdale, Royal Mid-Surrey and Berkshire. In away matches, we had the chance to sample these prestigious courses. Tommy's home venue is West Hill in Surrey, a charming gorse and heather course typical for that part of the country. On a sunny day, immediately after a morning ward round, a few of us would rush down to West Hill for a quick 18 holes. Our clubs were already stowed in our cars for a swift getaway.

The highlight of the year was the weekend at the beautiful links course at Rye on the Kent coast. This was the annual treat for the golf team by the consultants, many of whom were keen golfers. Indeed, one played regularly in the British Amateur Championship.

Besides golf, a group of us frequently went skiing together, visiting resorts like Klosters in Switzerland (Prince Charles's favourite haunt) to more humble ones such as Westendorf in Austria. I remember the Swiss resort of Verbier which was just a tiny village when we first discovered it, but is now a famous international venue.

On one of our skiing trips, there were four of us travelling together in one car. By some coincidence, three had long-winded double-barrelled surnames. When we arrived at the Austrian frontier, the officer had to record all our names. I could see he was becoming frustrated in having to spell all these out. When he got to me, the only brown foreigner in the group, he was expecting an even more formidable unpronounceable challenge. When he saw 'Loke', L-O-K-E, his face lit up. '*Ah, sehr gut!*' he exclaimed with relief.

Skiing is a risky sport. Apart from the occasional broken bone, we had always managed to avoid serious injury until one day when a tragic accident occurred. A member of the group crashed into a tree. He skied back to the chalet and seemed fine but did not join us for the afternoon skiing as he was feeling a bit tired.

When we returned, we found him unconscious. He was flown to the nearest hospital but it was too late to save him.

He had a subdural haematoma. This condition is often associated with a period called *lucid interval* when the patient appears normal. It is only when the bleeding has accumulated to such an extent as to cause serious pressure on the brain that the patient lapses into a coma. That is why all cases of concussion must be monitored closely to detect any deterioration in the patient's condition. We were all medical students and should have known about this and kept an eye on him, but we had forgotten all we had learnt.

I continued to ski with my family into my late 70s but decided that the prospect of a broken bone at that age was not an option. The arrival of snowboarders has increased the chance of an accident. They dominate the piste and are frequently out of control.

When we get older and have small children, we don't need the razzmatazz of the glitzy ski resorts. The ideal place would be one which is easily accessible from the nearest airport without a tedious long car transfer. In the resort, the children should be able to ski directly from residence to the nearest lift without having to carry their skis. The resort should be sunny with plenty of snow. I settled on Isola 2000, a resort in the Alpes-Maritimes, a short 2-hour drive from Nice airport. It is a purpose-built resort with direct access to lifts from all the apartments. Being near to the Mediterranean, it is warm and sunny. It is high (2000 m and above) and set in a bowl with its own microclimate that captures snow lasting until late spring. Our children learnt most of their skiing there.

The ski area of Isola is small and compact. I could let the children out on their own, comfortable in the knowledge they would not get lost. I would hesitate to do this in the larger resorts like Zermatt (Switzerland) whose vast lift system connects to that in Cervinia (Italy) on the other side of the Matterhorn, so that you can start off in one country and end up in another. I once asked if I needed to take my passport!

One year, while skiing in Geilo, Norway, I saw someone negotiating a steep slope so elegantly I stopped to watch in admiration. Furthermore, the skier was wearing a cowboy Stetson instead of the usual ski helmet. As he came closer, I noticed he looked like a Chinese person. Now, an expert Chinese skier wearing a Stetson is not the usual kind of visitor one encounters in a tiny resort in the middle of Norway. Intrigued, I went up to talk to him.

Here is his story. Once upon a time, he was a tailor toiling away at some deprived area in London's East End. One day, he saw an advertisement for a ski holiday. He was so enchanted by the scene of sun and pristine snow, such a contrast from his own dismal surroundings, he decided to book a trip. He came to Geilo because it was the least expensive resort he could find, dressed in his 'home-made baggy pants', as he put it.

After one season, he was hooked. He returned every year until he became proficient enough to gain a ski instructor's certificate. Today, he runs a ski school in Colorado, hence his headgear. He still makes regular visits to Geilo, the place where his life was transformed.

What a wonderful uplifting story—a real-life fairy tale!

Tommy's had a flourishing car club. Its patron was the racing driver Archie Scott Brown. He was motorsport's first disabled driver. He was born with a malformed right arm and severe leg problems. Yet he won several races in his two-litre Lister-Maserati. Scott Brown introduced me to the Porsche car. This

Loading up the Porsche after a ski trip in France

was the beginning of my lifelong relationship with this make.

I bought my first one in 1961 and have driven the same make ever since. My present car, model 993, is now 28 years old. This is the longest period I have kept a car. It is the last of the Porsches with the iconic air-cooled engine. They are not made anymore. I will hand the car down to the next generation as a museum piece.

Penny and I have travelled all over Europe in our Porsche, from skiing trips in the Alps to summer drives through France and Italy. It is totally reliable and has never let us down. With its air-cooled rear engine and rear-wheel drive layout, the car is ideal for driving in snow and ice and can negotiate conditions on mountain passes where other cars fail. The final few kilometres before reaching a ski resort are usually steep and tortuous. Negotiating the sharp corners accompanied by the beautiful sound of the air-cooled engine in second gear echoing around the mountains is a sublime experience.

To me, the Porsche is not just a vehicle to take me from A to B. It is a moving sculpture that is timeless. An architect friend likens its shape to a used bar of soap where all the sharp edges have been worn away leaving behind a smooth rounded core—a brilliant image.

I enjoyed my clinical years at Tommy's. As my memoir shows, I remember more of the extracurricular activities than learning to be a doctor. I made more friends there than in Cambridge because many of us had similar interests. But London can be a lonely place. Unlike Cambridge where friends are no further than on the next staircase, in London they are scattered all over the metropolis. Arrangements have to be made to meet up. I had a small flat in Tavistock Square in Bloomsbury, a short car ride down Southampton Row and across Waterloo Bridge to Tommy's. Traffic was light in those days. Commuting was no problem.

A bachelor's degree of MB BChir allowed us to go into clinical practice. But before becoming fully registered as doctors, we had to undergo a year of housemanship in a hospital before being let loose into the world. The stars of the clinical years were given appointments at St Thomas' Hospital itself while others were dispatched to affiliated hospitals outside London. I was sent to a hospital in Essex called Black Notley where I met my future wife, Penny.

There is a neighbouring village called White Notley. During the Black Death in the Middle Ages, all the infected people were quarantined in Black Notley while White Notley was reserved for the healthy. They already appreciated the importance of isolating patients. The two villages still bear their original names and the hospital in Black Notley now stands on the same site as the one which used to house patients during the Black Death.

We were given more responsibilities in a peripheral hospital. The hierarchy had fewer layers than in a teaching hospital. Where I was, only one registrar was in residence. The consultant only visited occasionally. As a junior houseman, I was at the front line to deal with most things.

How to recognise a real emergency in the middle of the night was the most terrifying situation. Is a severe pain in the abdomen due to gallstones, kidney stones, ruptured appendix, peptic ulcer or an ectopic pregnancy? Should the case be dealt with immediately or could it wait until the next morning? I once woke up a consultant to tell him that a patient I admitted had died. 'You don't need me, you need God!' said he and hung up.

Tuesdays were scheduled for tonsillectomy. These were brutal forms of surgery with frequent post-operative haemorrhage. Finding a vein in a small child to set up a drip in the middle of the night was a nightmare. I dreaded Tuesday nights. But the experience I gained made me proficient in phlebotomy which is a useful technique to master.

Responsibilities were rewarded by being allowed to do some surgery. I removed an appendix all by myself. In theory, an appendix should just pop up through a small incision made at the right spot in the abdomen, the *McBurney's point*. But sometimes it can be difficult to find, as when it is tucked in behind a piece of intestine. My case was like that. It took me a long time to complete the operation, much to the irritation of the anaesthetist who kept on complaining throughout, 'Hurry up, I don't want to be here all day.'

I had to enlarge the incision in order to get my whole hand in to find the appendix. The patient, a young lady, was concerned there would be a conspicuous scar right above the bikini line. I had to reassure her (although not very confidently) that all would be well.

My year of housemanship persuaded me that clinical medicine is not for me. I prefer the laboratory environment where I am in control. At old student reunions, I am often ribbed by my clinical contemporaries: 'We treat patients while Charlie just sits and thinks!'

I have not wasted my medical degree. The training has given me an overview and better understanding of the purpose of my research. Adding clinical relevance to basic science is a valuable practical combination.

At the end of housemanship year, the carefree student days were finally over. Real life began.

7. Return Home

In the summer of 1960, I returned to Malaysia as a newly qualified doctor accompanied by a new wife—an English wife. Her name is Phyllis Elaine Penrice, known to everyone as Penny. She comes from a coastal town in the Lake District, an area of England well known to tourists. I was captivated by her soft, melodic Cumbrian accent. She has largely lost it now after so many years away.

I met Penny during my year of housemanship. She was a staff nurse at the Black Notley hospital where I was assigned. On my first ward round, I was gazing at an X-ray with a puzzled frown when Penny happened to walk past. She paused, turned the X-ray the right way up and walked on, all without a single word to me. She was obviously experienced in dealing with newly qualified doctors fumbling their way in the real world of clinical practice. The X-ray was from a 2-year-old child. I had never seen one of such a young patient. I was looking at it upside down!

We were married in a registry office in London on 28 September 1960. We decided to sail back to Malaysia instead of flying. This would be our honeymoon. During the voyage, we were seated together with two Chinese passengers, a sweet middle-aged lady and a charming young student. We got on very well together. Soon afterwards, we received an invitation from the First Officer to join his table for the rest of the voyage. I presume this was because they noticed that Penny is European and should, by right, be upgraded in the seating plan (I had to be included as an appendage). Even in the post-colonial era of the 1960s, racial division still prevailed. The colonies may have found their freedom but colonialism was very much alive.

In the shipboard social hierarchy, invitations to sit at tables presided by a ship's officer are highly prized. But Penny politely declined the offer, saying that she was perfectly comfortable with her newfound companions and wouldn't think of abandoning them in mid-voyage—a courageous decision. Beneath her gentle demeanour, Penny has a steely core. I am very proud of her. Anyone who has read Somerset Maugham or E.M. Forster will be familiar with such a situation.

Penny had never been east of Suez. I could see she was excited and nervous at the same time. She must have been thinking, 'What would life be like over there?' As the boat travelled east, succeeding ports became increasingly alien—Gibraltar, Port Said, Aden, Bombay (this was where Penny caught the first smell of the East), Colombo. And then our final destination—Penang Island. At the entrance to the harbour is a fishing village with small wooden houses built on stilts over the water. I pointed out to her, 'The fourth house on the left is where we will live.' It was a joke but not knowing my background she believed me. The stiff upper lip began to tremble, soon followed by floods of tears that couldn't be held back any longer. This continued until we finally drove through the wrought-iron gates into our big house in Gurney Drive. She was surprised and relieved but very, very angry that I had played such a trick on her. For me, it was a nostalgic moment, coming home to a place I had left eleven years ago.

Now for Penny to meet my parents. How would they react? Parents are generally not happy to see their children marry out of their respective race or culture. I used to sing a song to Penny called 'Misalliance' by Michael Flanders and Donald Swann. It is about two climbing plants, the honeysuckle and the bindweed, but it is really a metaphor for the human condition. The honeysuckle spirals upwards in a clockwise manner, while the bindweed climbs in an anti-clockwise direction. Growing side-by-side around a window, they fell in love and decided to get married.

> To the honeysuckle's parents it came as a shock.
> 'The bindweed', they cried, 'are inferior stock.
> They're uncultivated, of breeding bereft,
> We twine to the right and they twine to the left!'

It is an astute social commentary. There are people who are offended by interracial marriages.

Much to my relief, the initial reaction of my parents was welcoming. I could see that they liked her. The relationship became warmer with each passing day. My parents organised a wedding feast and took us to Hong Kong as a treat. We spent Christmas there and Penny was introduced to the Hong Kong branch of the Loke extended family.

While in Penang, Penny met up with my maternal grandma who did not speak English. Dressed in her *nyonya* finery of *sarong kebaya* with the typical diamond brooches fastening the front of her blouse, Grandma sat quietly smiling and nodding to Penny, all the while chewing betel nut which was a habit for people of that generation, like smoking. Penny also sat there smiling in return. There was total incomprehension on both sides but the meeting appeared to be successful.

As a wedding present, my parents gave us a plot of land in Kuala Lumpur on which we built a house to our own design. This was our first marital home. It is in an idyllic location, within walking distance of the Royal Selangor Golf Club where I am still a member. Penny used to stroll there with the children, accompanying them for their morning swim. We had a comfortable lifestyle and thought we would be living there forevermore. But it was not to be.

My fault. When the Cambridge job offer came through I took it. I was restless, trying to find a purpose in my life. Many people wrongly assumed that it was Penny who was dragging me back to England. She had built up a very happy home in Kuala Lumpur and was heartbroken when we left. We still own our house. It is there waiting for our return. When will this be?

I have always wondered how our lives might have been if I hadn't accepted the Cambridge offer. The path we choose is not always in our hands. Fate can intervene. I am reminded of the film *Sliding Doors*, starring Gwyneth Paltrow, which tells the story of a young woman rushing to catch a train home. The plot splits into parallel universes. One, she makes her train and gets home on time. The other, she misses her train and gets home later than anticipated. What she finds at home in those two scenarios will result in two alternate lives.

Our eldest daughter was born in 1961 at the British Military Hospital, Kinrara, a small town on the edge of the jungle just outside the Malaysian capital. Britain still maintained a military base in the country at that time.

It might seem rather strange for a civilian to have delivered a baby in a military hospital. It was at the suggestion of Dr Macpherson, a Scottish doctor who was my parents' GP. He knew Captain Peter Bessell, the obstetrician at the military hospital who was pleased to look after Penny. Since we had only just arrived back in Malaysia, we were unfamiliar with the obstetric services available. We decided to take up Captain Bessell's offer.

For Penny, it was not a happy experience. The hospital was on the fringe of a dense tropical rainforest. The conditions were primitive. Dogs and other animals roamed the wards. There was no air conditioning. Both mother and baby slept under mosquito netting in the hot, humid air.

Being a British Military Hospital did have some benefits. Penny was looked after by nurses from the Queen Alexandra's Royal Army Nursing Corps. They provided a buffer against the jarring alien environment and gave Penny a feeling of being in a hospital back home in England.

Penny lost a lot of blood and needed a transfusion. She is rhesus-negative, a blood type rarely found in Asian people. If she were in a civilian hospital in Kuala Lumpur, it would have been difficult to obtain matching blood for her. Fortunately, there was a soldier from New Zealand with the same blood group training in the jungle. He was airlifted out by helicopter for a blood donation.

Grandfather Loke Yew was said to have consulted an astrologer who told him that the surname Loke would die out after three generations in my branch of the family. We have four daughters, Katherine Tracey Kwai Tien, Amanda Louise Kwai Lin, Tamsin Jane Kwai Fai and Imogen Claire Kwai Leng. Penny and I have discussed whether we should continue until we produced a son to prove the astrologer wrong or to capitulate and call it a day. We decided to capitulate.

Leaving aside astrology, what does science have to say? A question that has been debated frequently among reproductive biologists is whether there is immunological selection for boys or girls inside the womb.

Each ejaculation is made up of two populations of sperm. One population carries the Y chromosome which will give rise to

Penny with Tracey and Imogen, youngest and oldest daughters

Tracey and Alexander

Tamsin with her daughter Grace

Penny and I with grandchildren Grace and Moss

an XY male embryo after fertilising the egg, while the other has the X chromosome which will produce an XX female. If fertilisation by X or Y chromosome is random, we would expect an equal number of male and female embryos to be conceived. But this is not what happens. There is a preponderance of male over female at conception in a ratio of about 160 : 100. One theory is that the Y-bearing sperm is lighter and can swim faster, thus reaching the egg first.

At birth, however, the ratio reverts to almost an equal number of boys and girls, with a ratio of about 110 : 100. There is, therefore, an unequal loss of male embryos from conception to birth inside the uterus. Male foetuses have also been observed to be spontaneously aborted more frequently than female ones.

We don't know why the intrauterine environment is

At Tracey's wedding. From left to right:
Tracey, Penny, Amanda, Tamsin, Imogen

so inhospitable to the male embryo. The presence of a Y chromosome may be responsible. This makes the male embryo immunologically more incompatible with the mother compared to a female embryo who has a similar X chromosome as the mother.

Penny also has a rhesus-negative blood group while I am rhesus-positive. This additional incompatibility would further add to the burden of the male foetus and affect its intrauterine survival. Penny has had one or two early miscarriages. We often wondered if those were male.

Nowadays, the sex ratio has been skewed artificially. In China, the male to female birth ratio is as high as 124:100, presumably because their draconian one-child policy introduced in the 1970s has led to the selective termination of girls. India also has too many men. Almost half a million girls are said to be selectively aborted every year. What effects this disparity in sex ratio has on society remains to be seen.

Perhaps in future, preference for male offspring will become less important. Even among royal families, the requirement for a male heir to the throne is no longer obligatory. An extreme example of male chauvinism was Henry VIII who went to the extent of beheading Anne Boleyn, his queen, for failing to produce a son. She did, however, give birth to a daughter. The supreme irony is that this daughter eventually became Queen Elizabeth I, a rare example of an alpha female in a strictly patriarchal society. If only Henry had settled for a female heir right from the start, the tragic saga of his six wives could have been averted.

It is common knowledge that women tend to live longer than men. So, at both ends of the spectrum, from womb to tomb, the male of the species appears to be more vulnerable than the female. He is also frequently reminded that his Y chromosome is so much smaller than the female X. Some scientists think that the human Y chromosome will one day disappear altogether. These revelations remind men that they are, after all, the weaker sex in spite of being physically bigger and stronger than women.

In the Gilbert and Sullivan operetta *Princess Ida*, Lady Psyche sings:

> Man is coarse and man is plain—
> Man is more or less insane—
> Man's a ribald—Man's a rake
> Man is Nature's sole mistake.

So there!

In addition to the ability to discriminate between male and female embryos, scientists are considering the intriguing possibility that the womb's immune system might also distinguish sperm from different individuals according to their genetic make-up. This will allow a woman to compare sperm from different partners and to select a genetically suitable sperm to fertilise her egg. Who will she choose?

Evolutionary biologists believe she will choose a sperm with genes different from those in her egg. This ensures that the embryo created from their union will inherit dissimilar genes from each parent, thus avoid inbreeding. In this way, she subconsciously encourages genetic diversity in the next generation even before a baby is conceived. Nature has already pre-empted her choice.

The undesirable consequences of inbreeding are well known. The ultimate taboo is incest. In the tragic tale by Sophocles (496 BC), Oedipus gouged out his own eyes in remorse on discovering he had married his mother and fathered four children with her. The mother, Jocasta, hanged herself in shame.

Tutankhamen, the king who ruled Ancient Egypt in the 14th century BC, was a product of incest. His mother was his father's sister. This might explain King Tut's various deformities. Egyptian society in those days believed that incest kept the bloodline pure. They were unaware of the perils of inbreeding.

Animals frequently use smell to choose a mate. Mice can determine the genetic make-up of other mice by smelling their urine. Interestingly, they prefer to mate with those whose genetic profile is different from their own. Here, then, is another stage in reproduction, at the level of mate choice, that discourages inbreeding. This precedes the selection of sperm inside the womb.

Can humans choose a mate by smell? Experiments are difficult to design in humans but there are a few so-called 'sweatshirt observations' hinting that mate choice based on smell also occurs. Volunteers are asked to wear sweatshirts and keep them on over a period of two or three days. The shirts are then presented to members of the opposite sex who are asked which odour they regard as most pleasant. Subsequent genetic analyses reveal that the majority prefer the odour of individuals whose genes are different to their own. This preference is more striking in women. Evolution has equipped them with a mechanism to choose a genetically suitable partner. And she will choose, not by his appearance but by his smell! So, men, forget about those bulging biceps and washboard stomachs.

Mate choice is a fundamental reproductive strategy in the entire animal kingdom. It is the starting point in the process of procreation so we must make sure we find the 'right' genetic partner.

Olfactory cues may have a subliminal but significant influence on human sexual attraction of which we are unaware. The power of personal odour should not be underestimated. The ability to recognise and distinguish between benign and threatening odours has evolved because it is a key survival mechanism for many creatures. That it is also used in mate choice should come as no surprise. Even the advent of the perfume industry may not be enough to override this natural selection.

Reproductive biologists and perfume makers are both keen on smell and sexual attraction but the reasons for their interests are different. Biologists want to find out whether a person's distinct odour can act as a sexual enticement for a potential mate based on their genetic profiles. It is interaction between two individuals. The perfumers' aim, on the other hand, is to discover a universal fragrance which will confer immediate sexual allure on all those who wear it, such as the Lynx deodorant which promises to raise the level of 'masculinity' in otherwise wimpish males. There is also Calvin Klein's cologne Obsession for men, billed as irresistible to women. This one, at least, has some scientific merit, as the fragrance was originally based on *civetone*, a compound derived from the scent glands of the civet cat which has been shown to have a marked influence on the sexual behaviour of these animals. Whether it will work on humans is another matter.

In 2010, scientists from the University of Liverpool discovered a scent in the urine of male mice that is indeed irresistible to female mice. They named it *darcin* as a tribute to Mr Darcy, the hunky hero in Jane Austen's *Pride and Prejudice*.

The vagaries of olfaction as a mechanism for sexual attraction may soon be a thing of the past. Modern technology is taking over. A dating agency in California is offering a genetic test for potential partners which includes analyses of their respective gene profiles. They will then match up couples who have the optimal degree of disparity. Science has replaced Nature in mate choice.

Most of us will probably rate appearance over smell as being more important in mate choice. In humans, visual images understandably play a big part in early attraction between the sexes. 'Who ever lov'd, that lov'd not at first sight?' wrote Christopher Marlowe.

Couples today are increasingly dating online, where appearance holds the key to success. A flattering selfie will generate the most 'right swipes' of approval. Odour no longer comes into play. Technology has eliminated one of our important senses in mate choice.

In our contemporary acquisitive society, we might add wealth as another attraction in mate choice. This might appear to be somewhat cynical, but look at the world of the rich and famous. 'Money is like a sixth sense without which you cannot make complete use of the other five,' declared Somerset Maugham. He was a shrewd observer of human weakness which he explored in many of his novels.

My first job in Malaysia was at the Institute for Medical Research (IMR). I recall turning up at the Institute carrying my CV to enquire what's on offer. Fortune smiled on me that day. While I was in the front office, the Director walked in.

'What do you want?' he said.

'I have just come back from overseas and am looking for a job,' I replied.

He looked curiously at my CV for a long time. 'Hm. We could do with a junior pathologist. I think we can give him a job,' he said to the administrator in the office. And that's that. No formal interview. No further questions. This one tiny stroke of luck from a fortuitous encounter started my entire scientific career. What are the chances of an event like this happening in a lifetime? I have not been back to the IMR since I left all those years ago. I must visit the place again (if it still exists) and see if I can recapture some memories of that momentous day when everything came together for me.

The IMR is the central pathology laboratory serving the whole of Malaysia. All pathological specimens requiring diagnosis were sent there. The place was an excellent repository of archival material and records going back many years. It was here that I first encountered three intriguing conditions which would from the basis of my future research. One is *nasopharyngeal carcinoma* (NPC), a cancer of the nose and throat which I used as the subject of my thesis for the Cambridge MD degree (see Prologue). The second is *hydatidiform mole*, a peculiar abnormal development of the placenta. The third is *choriocarcinoma*, a cancer arising from the placenta. These last two ignited my lifelong fascination with the placenta.

Nasopharyngeal carcinoma is found mostly in South China. When a disease exhibits such a distinctive geographical distribution, it invariably invites a lot of questions. Are the Chinese genetically prone to develop NPC? Is there something in their lifestyle or environment that is especially unhealthy? Many theories have been put forward but so far we still do not have a definitive answer.

An intriguing proposal is that the cancer might be triggered by the Epstein–Barr virus (EBV) which is a member of the herpes virus family. But this virus is ubiquitous worldwide. In Western countries, people infected with EBV simply develop glandular fever, so why does the virus cause NPC in Chinese people?

Malaysia, whose population is made up of three main racial groups, Malays, Chinese and Indians, offers a good opportunity to compare the prevalence of NPC among them. Analysing the data from the IMR, I found that the cancer occurred predominantly among the Chinese who were originally migrants from South China. It seems that the susceptibility to NPC travelled with them even when they have left China for another country, which suggests there might be a genetic factor involved. I suspected it was probably something to do with differences in the immune response to the virus.

With so many questions still hanging in the air, I decided that NPC would be an interesting subject for my Cambridge MD thesis.

After a thesis is approved, the candidate has to appear in person to defend it in front of a panel of examiners. Since NPC is uncommon outside Asia, I was quietly confident (overconfident, as it turned out) that I had an advantage over my Cambridge examiners.

When I presented myself for the examination, I was shocked to see a Chinese gentleman seated next to the Cambridge Regius Professor who introduced him: 'I have taken the liberty to invite Professor Ho (I think that was his name), who is a leading authority on nasopharyngeal carcinoma, to listen to what you have to say.'

Totally deflated, I had to quickly pull myself together and maintain some composure. Fortunately, after a few hours of inquisition, the examiners were satisfied with my answers. I passed! I had now progressed from a Bachelor of Medicine (MB) to a Doctor of Medicine (MD).

My tentative entry into the world of scientific research was the simple observation that the majority of hydatidiform moles had two X chromosomes, indicating that female placentas were more prone to develop this condition. With great excitement I published this in the *Journal of Medical Genetics*, my first scientific paper in an international journal. Sadly, while I was correct in my observation, I was wrong in my interpretation. In science, as in other walks of life, appearances can be deceptive.

It transpired that the XX chromosome constitution is the result of a peculiar mechanism of gene regulation known as *genomic imprinting* which was only recognised in the early 1980s. In fact, all the hydatidiform moles are males and not females. This happens when an egg is fertilised by two sperm instead of just one as normally occurs. Since sperm is from the father, excessive *paternal* genetic input tilts the balance towards development of a hydatidiform mole. Too much father is bad! This is because genes from the father and those from the mother behave differently.

The mule shows this clearly. It is a cross between a female horse and a male donkey. But the reverse cross between a male horse and a female donkey will produce a hinny, an animal totally different from a mule. Both have the same combination of parents and inherited the same mixture of genes, and yet they are different. This has been a puzzle ever since mule breeding began in ancient times. Homer (800 BC) described it in the *Iliad*. Now we know the answer. Who is the father and who is the mother is crucial, a phenomenon referred to by geneticists as *parent-of-origin effect*. This is an important point to consider when studying human reproduction.

Choriocarcinoma is equally intriguing. It is a cancer that has originated from the placenta. The placenta is an organ that is part of the baby. All cancers normally arise from our own tissues. Choriocarcinoma, therefore, is unique in having arisen from another person's tissues (the baby's). The normal placenta has very similar characteristics as its malignant counterpart. They are but two ends of a spectrum.

From the IMR, I was recruited as a lecturer to the newly established medical school in the University of Malaya (UM). At that time, I was in London awaiting the birth of our third daughter, Tamsin. The Dean of the Faculty of Medicine in UM wanted me to start immediately as the new cohort of students was about to arrive. I was in a dilemma. The sensible thing to do, of course, was to stay in London with Penny for the birth, but in my excitement to start my new job, I chose to go, leaving Penny to fend for herself in London. I have never forgiven myself for this contemptible selfish decision.

Worse was to come. On the flight home, Penny's plane had to make an emergency landing, with foam sprayed over the runway and fleets of ambulances in attendance awaiting potential disaster. I can imagine how frightened Penny must have felt, alone with a newborn baby braced for emergency landing. And I was not there with her! For many years afterwards, Penny refused to fly.

This whole episode is a serious black mark in my life. Penny and I seldom talk about it. What should have been a joyous occasion has become something that is best forgotten. And all because of that fateful decision I made.

8. On The Road

Academics tend to travel widely, attending conferences and giving lectures. This is an important part of the job. They can be fun. It is not always all work and no play. The winter meetings at Banff in Canada, for example, were organised in such a way that lectures took place in the morning and evening while the afternoon was left free for skiing.

I even took my golf clubs with me on some occasions. At a meeting in the University of Rochester, New York, I was invited by Professor Henry Theide to play a round with him at the exclusive Oak Hill Country Club which has hosted the Ryder Cup and PGA Championships. Organisers of a conference at Glasgow University arranged for me to play at the famous Gleneagles golf course. I've also had enjoyable games on the courses around Sydney during meetings there. On one occasion, when the day's programme wasn't all that interesting, I tried to sneak out for a round early in the morning. Unfortunately, I met the organiser of the conference coming down in the same hotel lift. 'Ah, Charlie, we won't see you today then,' he said with a forced smile.

Cornell has its own golf course on campus. It was always a pleasure to give a seminar there and play a round with my old friend, Professor Doug Antczak. He is an equine reproductive biologist. The horse placenta, surprisingly, has many features similar to those in our own.

To be asked to give the keynote lecture at an international conference is the ultimate accolade. But to get there, one has to start at the bottom. The first step is to put up posters in the reception area illustrating one's research. We have to stand by the posters waiting to answer questions from anyone who is interested, like a vendor selling goods from a stall. It can be soul-destroying if nobody stops to buy.

Hopefully, this will be followed by invitations from conference organisers to give a short podium presentation. If judged to be a good speaker with interesting data, one is eventually promoted to the plenary session, which either opens or closes the conference.

I have been through all these stages.

When my first book *Immunology and Immunopathology of the Human Foetal-Maternal Interaction* was published by Elsevier in 1978, I waited anxiously for the reaction of the scientific community. A review duly appeared in the medical journal *The Lancet.*

> Scientifically this is an admirable book in every way for it deals with the subject clearly and sensibly. ... I find it greatly superior to its rivals mainly because it benefits from the authorship of a single and highly critical writer. ... Obstetricians, gynaecologists and immunobiologists interested in reproduction and development will find this book of great interest.

This was encouraging, especially as the reviewer was Leslie Brent, who, in the 1950s with Rupert Billingham and Peter Medawar, established the immunological basis of transplant rejection (see Chapter 9).

I went to my first conference shortly afterwards in Paris to gauge how the book had been received. There I met Rupert Billingham, the third member of the Medawar team. He looked at my name badge pinned to my jacket.

'Are you the Loke who wrote the recent monograph?'

'Yes, I am,' I replied.

'Why is it I have never seen you at a meeting?' he asked. 'You must go to all the important meetings and present your work. No matter how much you write, people must put a face to a name. Otherwise, you will soon be forgotten.'

I have taken this advice on board.

Meetings are also good opportunities for networking, a chance to meet the right people who might be useful allies in future. Who you know can sometimes be more important than what you know in the academic world. I am not very good at this. I have neither the charm nor guile to pull it off.

It can be stressful, giving a lecture to a highly critical audience made up of one's peers. To keep them interested for a whole hour is part science, part theatre. One has to 'perform'. After years of lecturing to undergraduates, I have learnt to judge how attentive they are from their body language. Are they following my presentation or are they glazed in the eye?

When I first started on the lecture circuit, I was encouraged by the positive response. I can recall one conference in particular. During the lunch interval, someone came up and congratulated me. 'It must take a lot of practice to deliver such an eloquent lecture.'

Lord Winston, the IVF pioneer who was chairing the meeting joined in: 'It is not a question of practice. You must have total command of your subject.' This kind of feedback is very important to help build up confidence. But some lectures can fall flat if the audience is unfamiliar with the subject. I once addressed 1000 paediatricians in Washington. The huge hall was dark with a single spotlight focussed on me. I couldn't see the audience but the light was just enough for me to pick out the front row. One person there caught my eye. His body language was unmistakable: he was fast asleep! How many more like him were out there?

Most of us have had moments of inattention when listening to a lecture. My own experience was embarrassing because I was caught out. The speaker had finished and was taking questions. My mind was wandering when I suddenly heard my name mentioned.

Vaguely I heard the speaker say, 'I'm afraid I don't know the answer. Perhaps Charlie Loke here in the audience might be able to help.'

All attention was directed at me. Sheepishly I had to ask, 'Can you please repeat the question?'

The dreaded part of a lecture is the question and answer session at the end. Most questions are genuine enquiries to clarify a point made. Others are what I would call 'trick questions', usually from rival factions, designed to confuse the speaker. We just have to learn how to deal with them. Occasionally, a session can descend into farce because of the language barrier at an international meeting.

Some Japanese professors have solved the problem by designating their junior colleagues to answer questions for them.

I once suggested to my own research group that I adopt a similar practice. I was told in no uncertain terms to do my own 'dirty work'. The rigid hierarchy of Japan cannot be transferred to Cambridge.

The style of presentation has changed since the arrival of PowerPoint. Now, many lectures are rapid flashes of illustrations on the screen. The message is mainly conveyed by visual projection. I am old-fashioned. I prefer to present my story verbally and only show pictures along the way in support of the narrative. I feel that this is more engaging for the audience, to allow them time to digest my arguments and conclusions and not pound them into submission with a visual bombardment. This is sometimes described as 'death by PowerPoint'.

Of all my travels, the one I treasure most is my trip to China with Penny in April 1983, sponsored by the World Health Organisation (WHO), to give a series of lectures on reproductive immunology at the Obstetric and Gynaecology Hospital in the Shanghai First Medical College.

At that time, China had still not fully opened up the country to foreign visitors after a decade of Cultural Revolution. My own country, Malaysia, did not allow its citizens to travel to China in case we became corrupted by communism. WHO solved this problem by issuing me with a United Nations passport. It was bliss to be able to travel unimpeded across continents.

Penny and I flew into Beijing where we had a chance to visit the Great Wall. It was a very emotional moment for me to actually walk on this iconic structure for the first time. As a young boy in Penang, Grandma once took me to a Chinese opera featuring the building of the Great Wall. It was an epic story told in song and intricate gestures, typical of this form of theatre. I have never forgotten the performance.

Our Chinese hosts provided us with a car, a driver and a guide, called Yin Yi, who accompanied us everywhere. We were not sure if this was a courtesy gesture or she was a spy to report on our movements. We were allowed to look inside the Imperial City which was normally closed to the public. I remember the car: a black sedan with curtains on the windows, like something

Penny and I on the Great Wall of China

Al Capone would ride in. There was no traffic on the roads. I am glad we saw Beijing and Shanghai at the time when 'Old China' still existed. Modern China is a different place.

The Obstetric and Gynaecology Hospital was staffed by a group of remarkable lady doctors. Some of them were graduates of prestigious US universities, like Harvard, Yale or John Hopkins. They were marooned in China during the Cultural Revolution. I don't know how they coped. The shelves in the museum were empty. All the pathology specimens collected over decades have been destroyed as they were deemed to be 'bourgeois'.

When I returned to Cambridge, I invited one of these doctors,

Doctor Li, to be a Visiting Fellow at King's College for one term. I hope she enjoyed her stay but I never heard from her or from any of the other doctors again. I wonder what's happened to them.

Doctors at the Obstetric and Gynaecology Hospital in Shanghai

The flight back from Shanghai to Hong Kong was memorable for being terrifying. There were more passengers than seats available, so China Airlines simply added extra portable chairs in the central aisle.

As a consultant in reproductive immunology for WHO, I have visited India many times. Scientists at the Institute of Immunology in New Delhi were trying to make an anti-fertility vaccine. The target was the hormone *human chorionic gonadotropin* (HCG) which is made solely by the placenta (see Chapter 9). The theory was this anti-HCG vaccine would disrupt the development of the placenta and, thus, prevent pregnancy. But it proved difficult to achieve in practice. After a few unsuccessful clinical trials, the project was abandoned. In retrospect, this was probably not a good idea in the first place. In disrupting pregnancy after conception has taken place, the vaccine is essentially an abortifacient rather than a true contraceptive. This might not meet with the approval of large sections of the community either for ethical or religious reasons. We still need to find an alternative method of birth control to the contraceptive pill.

I found India rather challenging. I never felt comfortable there. I re-read V.S. Naipaul's *An Area of Darkness* to see how he felt on his first visit to India, the land of his ancestors. Naipaul is a courageous author who sees the world as it is and dares to describe it truthfully. I sense he also had mixed feelings.

I was wary of the food and drink, fearing I might catch some disease. My concern was with those chronic infections, such as giardiasis, which tends to linger on even when treated. The usual advice given for travelling to places like India is to throw yourself completely into the experience or not to go at all. Penny managed to do the former and thoroughly enjoyed her stay. But I was more squeamish.

I did not normally take the whole family with me on my professional travels. I did once. In the early 1960s, the teaching of medical genetics was not yet an established item in the curriculum of medical schools. The WHO sponsored a course in this subject and invited selected universities from developing countries to nominate a member of staff to join the course at the Institute of Human Genetics in Copenhagen. I was chosen to represent the University of Malaya when I was teaching there.

In the spring of 1966, Penny and I left for Denmark with our three small children Tracey, Amanda and Tamsin, aged 5, 3 and 2 at the time, all of us squeezed into a tiny car together with our luggage. We drove from London to Copenhagen via the overnight ferry across the North Sea.

We were provided with a little bungalow in Hellerup, a small town just north of Copenhagen, which Penny made into a comfortable home. She even managed to give a dinner party there for our Danish hosts and the other participants on the course.

Armed with a Danish–English dictionary, Penny did her shopping at the local co-op. She was surprised to find everything so cheap until she discovered why. The prices displayed were for Danish citizens and not for visitors but none of the staff had the heart to tell her until much later when the manager explained the set-up.

Penny made friends with the local hairdresser (this is always the first port of call for ladies when travelling). He happened to be a Londoner who married a Danish wife and decided to settle in Denmark. They were a lovely couple. We were invited for lunch in their apartment one weekend. The meal was accompanied by an unlimited supply of Schnapps. I was unaware of the potency of this alcoholic brew and promptly fell asleep, much to Penny's embarrassment.

The genetic course was a great success. It plugged a serious gap in my knowledge. I still have the notes I took. The course director, Dr Morgens Hauge, was a brilliant teacher who guided us through the complexity of genetic inheritance in flawless English. It was easy to forget we were sitting in a classroom in Denmark. I learnt sometime later that he had died following a tragic accident falling off a ladder while working in his house.

On the first evening after our arrival, all the participants were invited to a get-together party. To my surprise, I noticed someone in the crowd sporting a Cambridge University Medical Society tie.

'I am also from Cambridge. What is your college?' I cornered him.

'King's,' he replied. He was Professor Alex Boyo from the University of Ibadan, Nigeria. What are the odds of two King's alumni from separate continents meeting up at the same event in Denmark?

King's alumni seem to crop up in the most unexpected places. I was once in a taxi taking me from Los Angeles airport to Santa Barbara where I was to give a lecture at a conference. The taxi driver and I had the usual conversation: where have I come from, what do I do, why am I visiting the US. He happened to be a PhD student at King's, supervised by Tony Tanner, a Fellow and a dear friend of mine.

I was puzzled why he was driving a taxi. He told me that the positive discrimination in favour of ethnic minorities was such that a white male with a degree was automatically relegated to the end of the queue when looking for employment.

We stayed in Denmark for about four months. The children were too young to remember much except for their rides on the toy trains at the Tivoli Gardens. We bought many Christmas decorations and nativity scenes from the famous store, Illums Bolighus, in Copenhagen. These are still with us and are brought out every year to festoon our Christmas tree.

It is only now when writing about our trip do I begin to appreciate the mammoth task Penny faced caring for 3 small children in an unfamiliar house in a foreign country. It helped that the Danes are very friendly and hospitable people. Our children played happily with the Danish children, who were rather puzzled why ours spoke only English. We enjoyed our stay.

The last plenary lecture I gave to an international audience was in Melbourne in October 2002 on the occasion of my retirement. I said then it was to be my final farewell lecture. I have kept my word. When one is no longer at the cutting edge of research, there is nothing new to say. 'When the curtains come down, it is time to leave the stage' is good advice. Famous scientists might be able to dine out for a while on work they have done in the past. But for most of us, it is best to make a clean break and move on rather than fade slowly into obscurity.

My retirement coincided with the dawn of a new century. Looking through my list of publications to prepare for my final lecture, I suddenly realised with some alarm and despondency that the bulk of my work already belonged to the previous century. I was way past my 'sell-by date'!

I have been out of the academic limelight and conference circuit for many years now, so I was surprised to receive an invitation out of the blue on 20 December 2022 to lead 'a conversation on the placenta' at a conference for Native and Indigenous Americans in Phoenix, Arizona. Sadly, at my age, I no longer have the energy for long-distance travel, especially in this COVID era. It would have been interesting to hear how these people deal with their placentas after birth. Different cultures have their own customs.

If we want to promote general interest in what we do, we need to engage the public and talk to them and not just to fellow scientists. I gave my first public lecture at the 10th Edinburgh International Science Festival on Sunday, 5 April 1998. My talk was sponsored by the British Society for Immunology. The organisers had cleverly inserted the enigmatic title 'Baby Transplants' in the printed programme, instead of the more scientific but bland 'The Foetus as an Allograft'. This drew a large crowd, curious about what I had to say.

The event caught the attention of the national press. Shortly afterwards, Hilary Bower from *Independent on Sunday* came to interview me in Cambridge and wrote a full two-page article entitled 'An Alien Under the Skin' (*The Sunday Review*, 19 April 1998). I am impressed she understood the complexity of reproductive immunology and fully grasped our idea that pregnancy involves an immunological system that is different from organ transplantation. She even managed to capture our excitement of having changed the prevailing paradigm.

> Dr. Loke ... outlines the new and controversial theory he and his eight-strong team have laid before the immunological community this year with the excitement of a group on the edge of a breakthrough. Thirty years a Cambridge don, he's careful to point out that it is a hypothesis, but one backed by accumulating evidence, and so elegant, he says, that it wakes him at night in his King's College rooms, soothed by the sigh of the River Cam.

A bit of journalistic licence, but I do have a lovely room in the Gibbs Building overlooking the river (see Chapter 5).

This was followed by the article of Virginia Blackburn, highlighting the need for more research on miscarriage, published in *The Express* on 10 August, 1998.

> 'The problem is that miscarriage is not considered a serious disease like heart trouble or cancer', says

> Dr. Charlie Loke, head of the University of Cambridge's research group in human reproductive immunobiology. Rather, people believe it is bad luck, so it doesn't arouse such an emotive response.
>
> Dr. Loke, who has been researching this area of research for more than 20 years, believes that problems occur because the placenta, which is the baby's life support system, does not implant itself into the womb properly, thereby causing the baby to die.

Corinne Podger, writing in the *Cambridge Evening News* (11 August 1998) echoed the need for more research on miscarriage.

> Research by a city scientist has been singled out to highlight a national campaign to raise cash towards understanding the tragedy of miscarriage in pregnancy. Dr. Loke said his team was trying to understand interactions between the placenta, which carries part of the father's genetic material, and the mother's womb. Rosalind Freeborn, of Tommy's Campaign, said we are very grateful for the work of people like Dr. Loke, because miscarriage is still seen as bad luck, and not enough is known about it.

One morning, our cleaning lady came to work very excited. 'I heard you on the radio!' she blurted. She had tuned into my interview about pregnancy and miscarriage on Radio Cambridge.

All this publicity sprang from just a single public lecture at the Edinburgh International Science Festival. The placenta has never managed to gain the public attention it deserves, despite its importance. It has always been the Cinderella organ languishing in the background. Maybe now it will have a ticket to the ball.

Another way to popularise the placenta is to write about it to a general audience. My first foray into popular science writing is *Life's Vital Link: The Astonishing Role of the Placenta*, published by Oxford University Press in 2013, followed by a softback edition in 2018. If the positive reviews in the media and enthusiastic comments from readers on the Amazon website are anything to go by, the book has certainly increased public interest in the placenta.

Nowadays, we have to be careful when talking or writing about the placenta and pregnancy. The culture wars are escalating and becoming increasingly toxic. Douglas Murray catches the prevailing mood in his book *The Madness of Crowds: Gender, Race and Identity*. As a reproductive biologist, the issue which concerns me most is the one of gender.

All this has led to the present situation where gender-specific nouns, such as 'man/woman' or 'father/mother' are being discarded. Pregnant mothers are now referred to as 'pregnant people' and 'father/mother' simply replaced with 'parent 1/ parent 2'. This is problematic when trying to understand human reproduction.

Changing a word here and there may be just a semantic quibble. But words are powerful. They reflect and shape reality. 'Beware this war over words,' warns the playwright Tom Stoppard. In reproductive biology we need to know who is responsible for shouldering the burden of pregnancy.

Giving birth to live offspring imposes a heavy burden on the female. She has to accommodate the unborn child inside her womb for a considerable period until it is ready to face the outside world. During this time, the female body is subjected to a series of upheavals, some of which are merely inconvenient but others might even endanger her health. Keeping the baby safe and fed inside her womb is not an easy task.

Even before a woman becomes pregnant, she has to make elaborate preparations in her womb to await the arrival of the baby. These changes coincide with the monthly release of an egg from her ovary. If pregnancy does not occur, all these modifications so carefully constructed are dismantled and discarded, only to be built up once more in time for the next ovulation. And so it goes on for the rest of the woman's reproductive life. This merry-go-round is the menstrual cycle, constantly moving between hope and disappointment.

A mother's duty does not end at birth. She continues to care for her newborn by breastfeeding and the nurturing that accompanies it, a process that is essential for the development of the infant's brain. Much of the expansion and maturation of the human brain takes place after birth, especially that of the forebrain, a vital part that endows us with our distinctive cerebral qualities. The nerve cell connections in this area are dependent on the quality of care the mother provides. Inadequate nurturing will disrupt this construction with dire neurological consequences.

After fertilisation, the sperm and egg each donates 23 chromosomes to make up the normal number of 46 in the embryo. But contributions from the two sexes are not equal. In the cytoplasm of the egg are tiny organelles called *mitochondria* which are passed on to the embryo. Sperm do not transmit mitochondria. We, therefore, inherit more genetic material from mother than from father.

An embryo's development does not depend solely on the genes it possesses. The characteristics of an embryo can be modified by the environment inside the womb, by a process known as *epigenetics*. It is a combination of Nature (the genes) and Nurture (the environment). A mother is passing on information about her own experience to her unborn child. In this way, she leaves a dual legacy behind.

The prolonged coexistence inside the womb before birth, together with the postnatal bonding afterwards, builds up a relationship between mother and child that is especially close. Mother makes us who we are.

Everything I have described takes place in the mother. Evolution of viviparity (giving birth to live offspring) has resulted in an unequal distribution of workload between the male and female parents. We should recognise this fundamental biological difference and not abolish a mother's identity. A mother is much more than just one half of a parental partnership.

Brave New World, the science fiction novel by Aldous Huxley published in 1932, tells the story of an imaginary dystopian society where the state exerts complete control over its citizens. In the World State, babies are made in laboratories and words like 'father' and 'mother' have become obsolete. And yet, the irony is that the Director of the Central Hatchery himself had an illicit liaison with a woman called Linda and 'fathered' a son. The urge to reproduce in the natural biological way was too strong to resist.

A similar theme is the 1965 Jean-Luc Goddard film noir *Alphaville* which depicts a godlike supercomputer called Alpha 60 who rules over a faraway galaxy. It manages the minds of its citizens by slowly removing words from the dictionary. An object will cease to exist if there is no word to describe it.

We seem to be already going down this route. The boundary between real life and science fiction is becoming blurred. Perhaps it has always been so. 'Fact and fiction are more connected than their separation on the shelves of libraries would imply,' maintains the literary critic John Sutherland.

9. Department of Pathology

Pathology is the study of disease. In most people's minds, pathology conjures up images of corpses in the mortuary. This is how the subject is portrayed in television dramas and on the big screen. There is a joke that does the rounds among medical students: 'A physician knows a lot but does very little; a surgeon knows very little but does a lot; a psychiatrist knows very little and does very little; a pathologist knows a lot and does a lot—but one day too late!' This further reinforces the perception that pathology is a post-mortem subject that comes into play only after death.

Pathology teaching in Cambridge is not like that. The Cambridge undergraduate course looks at what causes harm to the living, not what is found in the dead. The course caters for both natural scientists and medical students. The academic staff in the department reflects this. There are more biologists than medical doctors. We have no clinical responsibilities. Our job is to teach and engage in research, the perfect niche environment for me. The disparaging remark, 'Those who can, do; those who can't, teach', attributed to George Bernard Shaw, is a bit unfair. The two activities complement each other. Most of us will do both.

Cambridge medical students do a research project in their third year. This is an important adjunct to their lectures, to learn how to do things for themselves. 'I hear and I forget. I see and I remember. I do and I understand.' (Confucius)

As a newly appointed junior member of the academic staff in the department, my first task was to set up a research programme. What should I work on? When I was at the Institute for Medical Research in Malaysia before arriving in Cambridge, I had already developed an interest in the placenta, as explained in Chapter 7. I decided that this would be my research project.

In the early 1950s, Peter Medawar established that rejection of an organ graft (such as kidney, liver, or heart) was due to the donated organ being recognised as foreign or 'non-self' by the recipient's immune response. He was awarded the Nobel Prize for this discovery. At the same time, he asked, 'Why then is the baby not similarly rejected, since it is partly from the father and should, therefore, be regarded as 'non-self' by the mother?' This is the *immunological paradox of pregnancy*.

Over the following decades, reproductive immunologists have focussed on the interaction between the mother and her baby to find the answer to this paradox. Innumerable hypotheses were proposed but none stood the test of time. This is because we had been following a false trail. Focussing on the baby was a mistake.

There is no direct cellular contact between baby and mother throughout pregnancy despite the baby taking up much of the space inside the womb. All communications between the two are made via the placenta. In the context of immune recognition, it is how the mother 'sees' the placenta and not the baby that matters. We can no longer follow the model proposed by Peter Medawar. We need to think of a new concept, this time based on the immunological relationship between the mother and her placenta. The whole paradigm has shifted.

In addition to the *adaptive* immune response responsible for organ graft rejection described by Peter Medawar, we possess another immune system known as *innate immunity*. This has a more ancient origin during evolution and was already in use by invertebrates a long time ago.

The Australian scientist Macfarlane Burnet noticed that discrimination by the innate system is based on 'self' recognition rather than 'non-self'. Any cell or tissue that lacks 'self' molecules will be deemed to be foreign. Using 'self' as a template, an organ that does not conform to this image will be regarded as a foreign entity. The innate system, therefore, primarily detects the *absence* of 'self' rather than the *presence* of 'non-self'.

Scientific ideas develop in unexpected ways. During the period of the Cold War, the Swedish coastline was constantly spied on by submarines from different nations. The Swedish government encouraged the population to report sightings of these foreign submarines by issuing a booklet with illustrations of what these look like. With commendable lateral thinking, some bright official suggested that, instead of producing a series of pictures showing foreign submarines, why not issue just one picture of a Swedish submarine with the request that people should only report if they were to see a submarine that did not look like Sweden's own submarine. A Swedish scientist, Klas Kärre, noticed this and formulated the 'missing self' hypothesis for the innate immune response.

We believe that this innate system is the one that governs the relationship between a mother and her placenta. Pregnancy is the only natural situation when tissues from two genetically distinct individuals come together (placenta and mother). Clinical organ transplantation is an *artificial* situation created by modern medicine. It is reasonable to think that the immunological relationship between a mother and her placenta during pregnancy should use a more ancient innate immune system than that between graft and recipient as seen in contemporary organ transplantation. Mammalian pregnancy has evolved long before clinical transplantation arrived on the scene.

In 1987, Ashley Moffett, a consultant clinical pathologist at Addenbrooke's Hospital, came to ask me if she could join my research group to study a population of cells which she had seen in the uterus. She thought these might be *Natural Killer* (NK) cells. At first, I was hesitant because I had never before accepted a clinician with no laboratory experience.

But I decided to give her a trial, since NK cells at that time were beginning to attract the attention of immunologists.

I said to her: 'If these are NK cells, you will not go back to clinical work again.' I was right on both counts. Yes, these are NK cells and Ashley never went back to clinical pathology. She stayed on in my laboratory for the rest of her career. This was a brave decision, to give up a secure position with a lucrative clinical salary for an unknown future.

NK cells are part of the innate immune system. Their presence in the uterus lends further support for our view that this is the system a mother uses to recognise the placenta. In April 2002, we organised an international meeting at King's College, Cambridge entitled 'NK Cells and Reproduction', linking the two together for the first time.

Although the evidence so far suggests that uterine NK cells are involved in reproduction in some way, we are still not clear what they do. NK cells start to accumulate in the uterus during the later stages of the menstrual cycle in response to progesterone secreted following the release of an egg. They are, therefore, already in the uterus even *before* pregnancy occurs. They are present *in anticipation* of pregnancy rather than *as a result* of pregnancy. Are uterine NK cells produced by the mother to welcome the arrival of the placenta and not as a defence against the placenta? Or do they do both to provide a balance between acceptance and rejection which is essential for successful implantation? We have not yet managed to answer these questions.

Ashley and I have been very productive, publishing over 120 papers together. Successful collaborations can be tremendously beneficial for both parties. Two people working together can provide more than the sum of the two brains. An article in the scientific journal *Current Biology* entitled 'No Man is an Island' addresses this very point.

When I retired in 2002, Ashley took over from me as director of the laboratory. Ashley herself has now retired and has handed over the running of the laboratory to her assistant Margherita Turco. It is very gratifying for me to see that the work I started so long ago in the 1970s is still ongoing today in the same laboratory. And significant advances are being made.

The surgeon Roy Calne who pioneered kidney and liver transplantation was at the nearby Addenbrooke's Hospital when I arrived in Cambridge. Comparing the genetic make-up between donor and recipient using the technique of *tissue typing* is the first step in the procedure to see if they match. This would be a useful technique for me to study the relationship between the placenta (donor) and mother (recipient).

Valerie Joysey, the Head of the tissue typing laboratory, very generously allowed me a small area in her domain to learn how to 'type' the placenta. The technique is very complex and fiddly, using minute quantities of ingredients, delivered by a micro pipette into tiny wells. It took me some time to become reasonably competent. I was taught by a very pretty technician called Myla who was there to 'hold my hand', as it were, throughout the procedure. I used to look forward to my lessons. I managed to show that the molecules on the surface of placental cells will bind to receptors on NK cells, providing further evidence for potential interaction between the two.

Roy Calne and I became close friends because of our similar interests. Outside the laboratory, we discovered we were both keen tennis players. We spent many summer evenings together on the University lawn tennis courts at Fenner's. He was a very competitive opponent with an aggressive serve-and-volley game. After his retirement, Roy spent a lot of time in Singapore where we continued to meet.

In *Brave New World*, the science fiction by Aldous Huxley, eggs are fertilised by sperm in test tubes in the laboratory instead of inside mothers. Fiction is now reality after Robert Edwards, a Cambridge biologist introduced *in vitro fertilisation* (IVF). The first IVF baby, Louise Brown, was born in 1978. Since then, 2–4% of all births in Western countries are conceived in this way.

Robert Edwards was awarded the Nobel Prize in 2010. Because of the nature of his work, he met with considerable ethical and religious opposition. Many people were, and some still are, uncomfortable with the idea of creating a new human being outside the body. I would emphasise that only the fertilisation step takes place outside the body. The subsequent gestation is within the mother's womb. IVF is not ectogenesis.

Robert Edwards was the scientist who invented IVF and Patrick Steptoe the obstetrician who translated it into clinical practice. Besides these two, there was a third member of the IVF team. This was Jean Purdy, the research assistant who ran the laboratory. Experiments that involve long-term cell culture under strict sterile conditions require meticulous handling. One false move and the entire culture will be contaminated and the work is ruined. While Edwards provided the intellectual input and Steptoe made clinical use of the end product, it was Purdy who made sure the cultured embryos survived. Since my own research is also dependent on the successful culture of placental cells, I can appreciate the importance of someone like Jean Purdy in the team. Tragically, Purdy died of malignant melanoma at the young age of 39. When the story of IVF is told, the world has largely forgotten about her.

Every year during full moon in November, a spectacular visual display takes place on Australia's Great Barrier Reef. The vast colonies of coral beneath the sea simultaneously release clouds of eggs and sperm which float to the surface for fertilisation. The blue light of the moon acts as a signal to synchronise the coral's activity. Fish and amphibians also scatter their gametes indiscriminately into the water where they live in the hope that some will meet and fertilise each other.

In contrast, humans and other mammals have evolved *internal fertilisation*, whereby sperm is introduced directly into the female uterus during sexual intercourse. This is less wasteful and avoids the roulette of fertilisation. But this has not entirely solved the problem. Of the millions of sperm deposited in the vagina, only about 100 succeed in reaching their destination to rendezvous with the egg. The rest are lost along the way because there are innumerable hurdles inside the uterus which they have to surmount. Eventually, only one sperm manages to fertilise the egg. Altogether, there is a lot of wastage.

Sperm's intrauterine journey is a remarkable feat of navigation and endurance. I always think of it as being like Homer's epic story of Odysseus trying to get home to his native Ithaca after the Trojan War. Throughout his legendary voyages which took ten years, Odysseus was continuously harassed and delayed along the way. Hundreds of other warriors were also trying to get home but Odysseus was the only one to make it. All others perished, just like sperm's own journey. Somehow, I don't think sperm would take too kindly to the saying 'getting there is half the fun'!

Now, IVF has partly solved the problem by carrying out the entire fertilisation process outside the body. It is somewhat ironic that humans have taken millions of years to evolve internal fertilisation only to be beguiled by the idea of reversing the process with IVF.

Meanwhile, we should temper our enthusiasm that IVF is the solution to all our fertility problems. While fertilisation of an egg by sperm is relatively easy to accomplish in the laboratory, the resultant embryo frequently fails to implant when it is put back into the womb. This is why the present success rate of having a 'take-home baby' continues to languish around 30% depending on the clinic involved. Clinics frequently present their data as pregnancy rates rather than birth rates which gives a misleading view of success. Anyone choosing a clinic should scrutinise the small print.

Implantation is the job for the placenta. This is the critical phase in human reproduction. It is a tricky manoeuvre. The placenta has to burrow into the womb just deep enough to obtain nutrients for the embryo but not too excessively as to cause haemorrhage in the mother. This is where the mother's immune response towards her placenta comes into play. We still do not fully understand how this delicate balance is achieved. My colleague Ashley and I described the basic mechanisms involved in *Human Implantation: Cell Biology and Immunology* published by Cambridge University Press in 1995.

Mother is in control. She decides whether to accept the fertilised egg or to reject it if she thinks it is not viable. This makes good economic sense. To get rid of a defective embryo early is less costly in time and energy than to carry it for longer and then see it miscarry later.

In my book *Life's Vital Link*, I inserted a quotation from Shakespeare's *Macbeth*: 'If it were done when 'tis done, then 'twere well it were done quickly.' I thought this was very apt. But the editor thought otherwise. Scrawled on the margin of the manuscript in vivid red ink was 'You are just showing off!' I stood firm and managed to have the quotation reinstated, clearly visible on page 48.

The relationship between implantation and IVF outcome brought Bob Edwards and me together in Cambridge. I published many papers in *Human Reproduction*, a scientific journal he started.

Bob was one of my referees for promotion to a Professorship. A referee's unqualified support is crucial; any hint of 'if' or 'but' will immediately disqualify the candidate no matter how good the CV. I don't know what he wrote on my behalf but I will always be very grateful to him.

Cambridge has two kinds of professorships. One is the conventional Chair attached to being Head of a department. This will be transferred to the next incumbent who takes over the headship. The other is a Personal Chair (*ad hominem*). This is awarded to a specific individual whose research is considered by the University to be internationally competitive and who is a leader in the field.

I was in Malaysia when my secretary Jenny Connor phoned me from Cambridge.

'There is an official-looking letter from the University which could be about your promotion. Shall I open it or wait until your return?' 'It is quite a bulky letter. Maybe this is good news,' she added.

We decided she should open the letter. Her intuition was right. It was, indeed, good news. The University allowed me to choose my own title. I chose 'Professor of Reproductive Immunology' which best reflects what I do.

Robert Borland, an Australian scientist in the Department, taught me how to do tissue culture. For medical and ethical reasons, the placenta cannot be studied in its natural state inside the pregnant woman (*in vivo*). Experiments have to be carried out using cells extracted from the placenta and cultured in the laboratory (*in vitro*).

Most of my early years in research were spent in isolating and characterising these placenta cells in culture. One property of placenta cells is they secrete the hormone human chorionic gonadotropin (HCG) into the culture medium. This is the hormone used in home test kits to detect whether a woman is pregnant. I used to go regularly to a nearby chemist to buy these test kits to monitor the growth of the placenta cells cultured in my laboratory. After several visits, I noticed the pharmacist was looking at me with some interest.

He must have been thinking, 'Why is this man constantly buying pregnancy test kits?' I decided not to tell him the reason to maintain the mystery.

Although I managed successfully to keep the placenta cells alive in culture long enough to perform experiments on them, I could not propagate them to give rise to successive generations, what biologists refer to as *cell lines*. Over the years, many other investigators have tried and failed. At last, in 2020, Margherita Turco, working in the same laboratory I started in the Department of Pathology, has done it. The cells she grew, called *organoids*, will

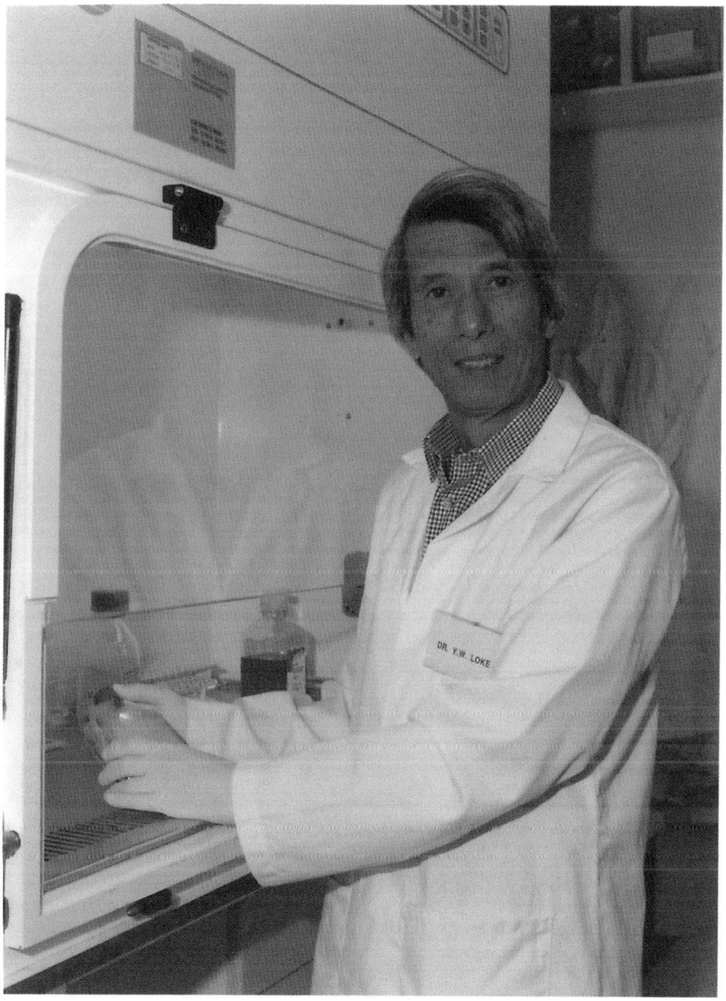

At the tissue culture cabinet

open up new avenues of research into placental biology. Margherita has also grown organoids from the lining of the womb (endometrium). For the first time, we now have the appropriate tissues to construct experimental models of human implantation *in vitro* that closely mimic the *in vivo* situation.

I remember many years ago setting the following question for an undergraduate Tripos exam: 'Future progress in placental biology is likely to be technical rather than conceptual. Discuss.' This has turned out to be true. The present generation has sophisticated technical tools that were not available to us in the past.

Bob Borland and I wrote many research papers together. When he retired from Cambridge, he went back to his family farm in Australia. The last time we met was in Melbourne in 2002, during the scientific meeting to mark my retirement. Sadly, he died of motor neurone disease in 2010 aged 77 before we could meet again.

I have unearthed some of the last letters we wrote to each other. We still communicated by handwritten letters in those days. By the autumn of 2009, Bob knew he was dying. We thought we might attempt to meet once more. He had gone to a great deal of trouble arranging a travel itinerary for me.

> We have lots of room at W-R, and would love to have you stay. We could meet you in Bairasdale (25km from Swan Reach). There is a direct train from Melbourne Southern Cross station to Bairasdale (approx. 4 hours). There is a 1.20 pm train departure which would mean your catching a flight out of Adelaide about 10 am.

I never made it. Yes, it is a long and complicated journey from Cambridge but I should have made the effort to go. In Chapter 1, I mentioned that one of my life's regrets are journeys not made. This is a glaring example. Penny accuses me of being lazy and selfish. I never put myself out. It is always the other person who is expected to make the concession. She is right; I admit this is a major character flaw.

In 2021, I sent a Christmas card to Bob's wife Ann in the hope we might establish contact again after all these years. I was uncertain whether her old address at their farm was still valid, so I was relieved that the card arrived safely. But it was received by Laird Borland, one of the sons, and not by Ann.

This is the return message he sent: 'I am sorry to inform you that mum died a couple of years ago.' Once again, I have left everything too late. Procrastination is another personal defect.

I used to make frequent visits to the Rosie Maternity Hospital with a bucket to collect placentas delivered at birth. These would be taken back to the laboratory where cells from the placentas were extracted and placed into tissue culture incubators. Examining full-term placentas allows us to look into what happens at the end of pregnancy. But the more important and interesting events, such as implantation, occur earlier in gestation. For this we need to use younger placentas, preferably from before the 12th week of pregnancy. These can only be obtained from elective terminations.

I have had innumerable meetings with the hospital ethical committee to seek permission to use these specimens. After a great deal of delicate negotiations, they finally agreed that we could proceed but under strict ethical guidelines. We were allowed to use only tissues from the placenta and not from the embryo. Permission must be sought from each patient and total anonymity maintained. These are sensitive and emotional issues but they are an integral part of doing research on the human placenta. Getting a regular supply of young placenta tissue is crucial. This is entirely dependent on the goodwill of patients and the cooperation of hospital staff. Otherwise, all projects will grind to a halt.

When placentas are collected, they need to be processed immediately, or the cells will die. Frequently, specimens become available at inconvenient times, like late on a Friday evening. Dissecting the placentas, disaggregating the cells and planting them onto tissue culture dishes can take many hours. The job requires a dedicated technician who is willing to put up with flexi hours. I was fortunate to have such as person. Lucy Gardner joined my research group at the very beginning and stayed with me until I retired. Always smiling and uncomplaining, Lucy was a vital member of the team.

In the early 1960s, the Department of Pathology in Cambridge was at the forefront of immunology research, due largely to the presence of Robin Coombs who invented the Coombs test for rhesus incompatibility. The rhesus blood group is a molecule found on the surface of red blood cells (like the more familiar ABO blood groups). The human population is divided into those who have this molecule on their red blood cells (Rh^+) and those who do not (Rh^-). If an Rh^- mother bears a Rh^+ baby who has inherited this molecule from a Rh^+ father, she might make antibodies against the baby's Rh^+ red blood cells because she will see those cells as foreign. These antibodies could destroy the baby's red blood cells resulting in the serious disease called *haemolytic disease of the newborn*. Coombs test is used to detect the presence of these antibodies in the mother's blood. If a rising level of these antibodies occurs, the pregnancy must be monitored very closely.

Lucy Gardner

I am Rh^+ but my wife Penny is Rh^-. Throughout her pregnancies with our four children, her blood was constantly monitored for the presence of antibodies by the Coombs test. Fortunately all was well.

Shortly after we arrived in Cambridge, Penny was introduced to Robin Coombs at a departmental party. She was very excited to meet the man himself who invented the test she had known throughout her pregnancy.

'I thought you were dead!' she gushed.

'As you can see, I am very much alive,' Coombs replied calmly.

Coombs got the idea for his test when he was still a young scientist.

I remember the Department of Pathology with great affection. It has been my academic home for most of my life. Without the support of the department and the people there, my story would have had a very different ending. When my post as Demonstrator came to an end, the regulations stated that I must leave unless I was promoted to a Lectureship. The Department wished to keep me. To do so, they had to offer me a Lectureship.

But there was a problem. It was not Pathology's turn to be allotted a Lectureship. Other departments had a greater claim. My department fought hard in the subsequent negotiations. The University finally decided I could be promoted only if Pathology were willing to sacrifice its next available Lectureship. My department agreed.

This was how I became a tenured member of the department. I stayed for 35 years until my retirement in 2002. Unlike some universities, Cambridge still has a fixed retirement age at 67. Louis Armstrong ('Satchmo'), the famous American trumpeter said: 'Musicians do not retire. They stop when there is no more music inside them.' Should academics be allowed to do the same until they run out of ideas?

I enjoyed teaching. I think I am quite good at explaining things. My lectures were generally well received. At the end of each term, the Department distributes questionnaires to all the students asking them how they rate the lectures according to content, interest and delivery, with a box at the end where they record a score of 0–10. My rating was frequently in the region of

8–9, with even an occasional 10. At least the consumers were satisfied.

For many years, I was given the honour to deliver the introductory lecture for the pathology course. Traditionally, this is a job for the Head of Department but the teaching committee wanted me to do it.

On a recent visit to Addenbrooke's Hospital in 2022, the consultant there greeted me: 'Professor Loke! You taught me in the early 1980s. I enjoyed your fascinating lecture series on inflammation. I can recall the memorable phrase you used, "pus, pus, laudable pus" and the 4 cardinal signs, "rubor, calor, tumor, dolor".' He could recite all this in such detail even though it happened over 40 years ago! A nurse nearby said, 'You must have made a big impact.'

I put a lot of effort into preparing my lectures. So it is a nice feeling that sometime, someone, somewhere remembers some of it.

Delivering a lecture for the first time to over 400 raucous students can be a terrifying experience. I remember my own student days when we were beastly to any lecturer we perceived to be weak and ineffectual. Their lectures were frequently disrupted by loud chattering and flying paper darts.

On one occasion, a lecturer was so distraught he fled from the hall. Except he didn't go through the exit door but into the broom cupboard instead! We waited quietly to see what would happen next. After several minutes, he crept out gingerly, thinking we had all gone, only to be greeted by howls of laughter. We were so cruel!

How did the students treat me? My technique, developed over the years, was to stand and stare silently at the audience to show that I was not intimidated. If the noise in the hall subsided spontaneously without my having to shout for silence, that was a good sign. Slowly, the students would focus on me and begin to listen. That was when I would start my lecture. If what they heard was sufficiently compelling, they took notes. I knew then I had hooked them and could reel them in. It was a constant battle of wits.

When I retired, the Department presented me with three leather-bound volumes containing all my published scientific papers with a dedication by the Head of Department, Professor Andrew Wyllie. I have included this in full.

DEDICATION

It is with great pleasure, but also a hint of sadness, that I undertook to write a short foreword to this remarkable collection of 170 scientific papers. The pleasure comes from seeing, put together, the scientific works over some 35 years of a man of great intellectual curiosity and persistence, a true pioneer in the field of trophoblast biology, a wonderful communicator and a delightful colleague. The sadness of course comes from the fact that these volumes are part of a collective goodbye from the Department to which Charlie Loke gave so much for so long.

All of these papers are of high quality: well-written, beautifully illustrated, provocatively discussed. Some are real classics. Amongst them must be counted the description of culture of human trophoblast (which opened a new field), the papers describing the unusual MHC molecules expressed by trophoblast and the identification and characterisation of the distinctive maternal lymphocytes (uterine Natural Killer Cells) found at the implantation site. But there are no weak links in this chain of papers. They are part of the knowledge base of human placental biology, the product of decades of thoughtful investigation, read and re-read by hundreds of scientists, and cited in all over 7000 times. Viewed together these papers demonstrate that facts and data themselves are not enough—although the facts are certainly there. But these are the basis for a constant stream of changing concepts and ideas which challenge existing paradigms, even those emerging from Sir Peter Medawar.

As well as charting Professor Loke's thought over the

years, these papers also show something of the size and variety of his extended scientific family. Within the authorship in these volumes lie a great many names. Some of these are close, long-term colleagues like Ashley Moffett, Sue Hiby and Lucy Gardner, but amongst the others are clinicians, post-docs, research assistants, and graduate and undergraduate students who worked with Charlie for a period only. Some of his co-authors were, at the time of writing, already well-known figures in reproductive biology. Others became so later. But none can have been unaffected by his abiding fascination with the unusual events on the borderland between fetal and maternal environments, or left in doubt as to the importance of the cause of reproductive immunology that he eloquently championed.

Those of us who worked with Charlie cannot read these papers without hearing his voice (so familiar as the introduction to pathology itself for decades of Cambridge undergraduates), or seeing his expression, alternating characteristically between intense gravity and irrepressible glee. His enthusiasm knows no boundaries. His personal charm is unique. Although I came to know him only in his last four years before retirement, he always seemed young to me. This Department is a large one and not short of strong personalities, but we shall be the poorer on the day our Professor of Reproductive Immunology enters the ranks of the emeriti.

So this three-volume collection is now coming home. The papers were typed by Jenny Connor, Charlie's loyal secretary for more than twenty years. It is a gift to its author from all his colleagues in the Department of Pathology at Cambridge.

Will it be used to prop up a lamp-stand in a gracious home in Penang? Will it stand in a stately bookshelf in England? Whatever, we hope that its owner will sometimes turn its pages and feel the satisfaction of the skilled artist who meets his own handiwork, years after its creation. Perhaps, Charlie, these papers will remind you also of the trials, excitements and rewards of years in the lab and of the people who shared these with you. We want to say a big thank you and to wish you a long, sunny, refreshing retirement.

Andrew Wyllie, June 2002

Reading it always makes me very emotional because it captures my years in the department so vividly that I can relive my life there all over again.

My retirement carried mixed feelings. One was relief to be free from the perpetual grind of research grant applications. The other was sadness. It marked the end of a chapter in my life that had been very precious to me. I missed my environment; I missed my friends; I missed the camaraderie of scientific research. And not to forget all those bright young minds who kept me intellectually alive over the years.

My research team at the Department

10. Reflection

After I retired and no longer engaged in research, I have continued to follow developments in the field of human reproduction.

Creation of the placenta is a pivotal milestone in the evolution of reproduction because it enabled humans and other mammals to give birth to live offspring instead of laying eggs like our reptile ancestors. It has taken over 300 million years to make this changeover. What innovations will we see in the coming years that will make a further impact on the way we reproduce?

Modern technological interventions have already reached into many corners of human reproduction, especially in the female. Science has given women the opportunity to determine their own reproductive destiny. The woman can now have sex without conceiving or to conceive without having sex, a privilege not available to earlier generations. Female reproduction has entered a brave new world.

Women are encouraged to freeze down their eggs when they are young to be used in future if needed. Companies such as Apple and Facebook have offered to pay their female employees the cost of freezing their eggs. Surprisingly, this apparent generous gesture has stirred up powerful emotive reactions. Critics denounced it as a ploy to pressurise female employees to delay having children and to focus on their job. The message sent out is that their career prospects could be jeopardised by the inconvenient onset of motherhood. The 'pram in the hallway' would be an impediment to career progress.

Unfortunately, in a highly competitive world, taking maternity leave, no matter how efficiently it is organised, could be disruptive, especially in scientific research. The first to publish gets the prize. To keep eggs frozen until an appropriate time to have a baby would give women a way out of this dilemma.

An alternative to freezing her own eggs is to procure an egg from a younger woman. But a mother then conceives a child who is not related to her biologically. She has forfeited her chance of propagating her own genes to the next generation. Instead, she is transmitting the genes of another person. But a woman who is desperate to have a baby is unlikely to be too bothered with this esoteric biological consideration.

Not all women fall for the siren song of the fertility industry. In an honest account of her own predicament, Amanda Platell, one-time press secretary to William Hague, the then leader of the British Conservative Party, described her despair when told that, at the age of 40, she would not be able to have a child unless she used a donor egg. But she did not want to carry 'an anonymous other woman's child'. In spite of her longing to be a parent, she accepted the biological fact that she would be childless.

There is an important practical issue relating to the use of a donor egg. As pointed out in Chapter 1, in the absence of mother's 'self' gene, pregnancies are more prone to complications, such as miscarriage, stillbirth or pre-eclampsia. About one in four women will suffer from pre-eclampsia after egg donation.

With egg freezing and egg donation, a woman's fertility is no longer constrained by her ageing ovary. 'Fertility beyond the menopause' is the kind of seductive headline seen in the media, with examples of women having children in their 60s and 70s.

This might seem to be a triumph of science over the laws of Nature but not everyone is comfortable with this development. In fact, most people are not. A European commission study asked more than 20,000 people in 25 European countries what they think. The vast majority (96%) said that the average maternal age should be limited to 42. In the Netherlands and Belgium, legislation limits treatment to women age 45 or younger.

There are valid reasons for such concern. Complications of pregnancy are more common in older women. There is increased likelihood of maternal illness and infirmity while the child is still young, and the wide generation gap between mother and child is also not ideal. 'Children and teenagers need their parents to look after them, not the other way round,' according to Professor Geeta Nargund, medical director of Create Fertility in the UK.

Even posthumous pregnancies are now possible. A terminally ill woman can freeze down her eggs. After her death, the eggs can be fertilised by her partner's sperm using IVF and the resultant embryo carried to term by a surrogate. The couple can now have biological children in the absence of one partner. Or even in the absence of both partners if they have the foresight to freeze down their respective eggs and sperm during their lifetime. The dynasty can then be extended into the future. Occasionally, the mother of a dead woman has been known to volunteer to be the surrogate, in which case she will gestate and give birth to her own grandchild—a novel approach to family dynamics.

From egg donation, we now have embryo donation. Over the years, the fertility industry has accumulated large numbers of unused embryos created by IVF which are surplus to requirements. These are now offered to infertile couples. The recipient mother is essentially adopting a child except that this is done before the baby is born and she herself provides her womb for gestation. She is acting as a surrogate.

Inevitably, there will be further modifications. Some clinics have gone beyond embryo *donation* to embryo *creation*. The clinic buys eggs and sperm from selected donors, fertilises them in the laboratory and sells the embryos to prospective couples. These are no longer surplus embryos but are embryos made to order by the clinic. The commissioning couple can request features they would like the baby to have.

Choosing eggs and sperm based on the characteristics of donors in the hope of producing a child with similar traits is notoriously unreliable. One is reminded of the exchange between Isadora Duncan and George Bernard Shaw. Isadora suggested they should have a child who would have her looks and Shaw's brains. 'But what if it had your brains and my looks?' was Shaw's response.

The technological goal is now more ambitious and has moved on from giving infertile couples a helping hand in attempts at producing healthier babies. *Preimplantation* and *prenatal genetic diagnoses* are two procedures that can help by screening embryos and foetuses for genetic abnormalities. A simple blood test using foetal DNA circulating in maternal blood is beginning to replace the previous invasive amniocentesis and chorionic villus sampling procedures with their associated risk of miscarriage.

The foetal DNA blood test is now so sophisticated that soon the whole genetic make-up of the embryo or unborn child will be on view to the parents. They will then have the choice whether to use the embryo for implantation or to terminate an existing pregnancy. In a way, this kind of selection is producing designer babies, but it is not eugenics. The techniques do not manipulate the genomes of future generations. They give parents the chance to choose a healthy baby rather than a genetically abnormal one. China is pursuing this type of screening in a big way. The country aims to identify all known genetic mutations and to eliminate them in future generations, thereby creating a healthy population. The technology is available to fulfil such a dream.

As the technology broadens to take in more and more genetic disorders, there will come a time when parents are overwhelmed by a profusion of genetic data, the implications of which they may not fully understand. Parents will need guidance from professional genetic counsellors to help them come to a decision. Having a baby will become intellectually more challenging.

Genetic mutations that cause serious diseases are the obvious choice for elimination, but what about those that are not life-threatening, such as Down's syndrome? This is where reason and emotion come into conflict. In a survey in Britain, 90% of women who are diagnosed with a Down's syndrome baby choose to terminate their pregnancies. Iceland has not had a baby born with Down's syndrome for over five years and Denmark is about to follow the same trend. Society in these Scandinavian countries have accepted the idea of fetal selection. Ultimately, progress in artificial reproductive technology is 'more defined by public acceptability than by the technology itself', according to obstetricians Fauser and Devroey in *Baby-Making*.

From screening for genetic mutations we now have the technology to correct or replace faulty genes in an embryo while still inside the womb using *prenatal stem cell therapy* or *prenatal gene therapy*. Both these procedures are still in the experimental stage. Their safety and efficacy have not yet been confirmed. Nevertheless, scientists are hopeful that genetic screening together with gene or stem cell therapy will one day free the world from the blight of inherited genetic disorders.

The new gene editing tool CRISPR-Cas9, invented in 2012, has increased the range of available methods for genetic manipulations. Like the others, the technique seeks to correct gene mutations in an embryo during its early development so it will be born without genetic defects. But the technique's ability to target other genes besides the defective one means it can potentially alter the entire genome of the embryo. These changes are inheritable and will be transmitted to future generations, ultimately becoming part of the human gene pool. Once introduced, these changes cannot be removed. We will rewrite the human genetic code. This is the greatest worry for most people and raises important ethical questions.

Science may be taking over from Nature in directing human evolution. Every life form inhabiting our planet today has evolved by natural selection. Now for the first time in the 21st century, we have the technical knowledge to break the laws of natural selection and replace it with intelligent design.

Attitudes among scientists vary from enthusiastic exponents,'if we can, then we should', to the more cautious 'just because we can doesn't mean we should'. With every new technical innovation, there is always this uneasy compromise between what science can do and what it should do.

Yuval Noah Harari, in his thought-provoking book *Sapiens: A Brief History of Humankind*, offers a timely warning when he concludes: 'We might fiddle with *Homo sapiens* to such an extent that we would no longer be *Homo sapiens.*' A possible scenario is that humans might be divided into different ranks within society as in *Brave New World* or even split into several subspecies.

At present, the use of CRISPR-Cas9 is strictly regulated, but once the technology becomes freely available, it will be difficult to patrol. There is already a breach. A Chinese scientist, He Jiankui, shocked the scientific community when he announced the birth of two CRISPR gene-edited girls at the Second International Summit on Human Genome Editing in Hong Kong on 18 November 2018. He did his experiments secretly. Even his own university was unaware of what he was doing. This illustrates the difficulty in reining in this technology. It is likely that more gene-edited children will be created in the future. Dr He himself hinted that he has already made a third. He has opened a Pandora's box.

Will human cloning become another form of assisted reproductive technology? Many animals have already been cloned since Dolly the sheep in 1997. The successful cloning of two monkeys by Chinese scientists brings cloning of humans a step closer. Who would want to do this? To replace a beloved lost one would probably be a prime motivation as it has already been done for favourite pets. Some vain celebrity, mad scientist or despotic dictator might like to create a copy of themselves in a futile attempt at immortality. They should be reminded that a clone is not an exact replica. Those who think they can reproduce an identikit of 'self' will be disappointed.

At present, human *reproductive* cloning, that is the creation of an identical individual, is forbidden in many countries. But *therapeutic* cloning is usually permitted under strict regulation. This is the creation of embryos from which stem cells can be harvested to treat a variety of diseases. For this, the embryo has to be sacrificed. To create something and then deliberately destroy it might seem to be a rather dubious practice. Both types of human cloning raise huge ethical questions.

Even cutting-edge technology still relies on an egg and a womb to complete the procedure. '*Ex ovo omnia*'—everything comes from an egg, declared William Harvey (1578–1657) in his thesis on animal reproduction first published in 1651. Human eggs are difficult to come by, so researchers are experimenting with animal eggs for eventual human cloning. They will transfer the nucleus from a human cell into an animal egg recipient whose nucleus has been removed. Since the clone produced in this way will comprise human genes from the nucleus and cytoplasmic genetic material from the animal egg, it is termed a *cytoplasmic hybrid* or *cybrid*.

More than 60 years ago, in 1960, two scientists, Manfred Clynes and Nathan Cline, coined the term *cyborg* (cybernetic organism) to describe an individual who is part human, part machine. The scientists contemplated the challenges that might lie ahead when humans set out to colonise extraterrestrial worlds. They would need to incorporate artificial devices which enhance their biological capabilities. Cyborgs became staples of science fiction, such as *The Six Million Dollar Man, Bionic Woman, Robocop* or *Iron Man*. Terminator as played by Arnold Schwarzenegger is best described as an *android* since he is an alien and his outer human appearance is merely a disguise. Cyborgs have now emerged from science fiction into the real world. Many people today have mechanical implants inside them that can influence a variety of bodily functions—a well-known example is the cardiac pacemaker. Anyone with it is a cyborg. Bionic limbs are also becoming available. With the arrival of cybrids and cyborgs, we humans may have to re-evaluate who we really are.

The technological innovation that is likely to have the most profound impact on the future of human reproduction is the ability to make eggs and sperm from skin cells by *in vitro gametogenesis* (IVG). This has already been achieved in mice. Women with fertility problems can then have eggs made from their own skin cells rather than go through the laborious and expensive process of stimulating their ovaries and retrieving their eggs. The technique will also help male infertility. An unlimited supply of eggs and sperm will become available.

Looking further ahead, if every individual is able to generate either eggs or sperm from their skin cells, there is no longer any need to have males and females for sexual reproduction. Same-sex couples can fertilise each other using gametes derived from their respective skin cells to create biologically related offspring.

Virtually all animal species are *dioecious*, that is they have males and females, according to evolutionary biologist Daphne Fairbairn of Princeton University in her book *Odd Couples*. Might humans evolve away from this ancient pattern of sexual dimorphism?

Why there are males and females has long been one of the major mysteries of biology. Procreation is perfectly possible without the division into the two sexes. In fact, it would be more efficient. The advantage is that you don't have to limit your choice of mate to one half of the population. Anyone will do. So why bother with having males and females?

The precursor to sexual reproduction probably occurred about 2 billion years ago when two sexless organisms met up and swapped genetic material. Bacteria now continue to do this by a process known as *conjugation*.

Over time, the partners evolved into two mating types. One partner started to make many small gametes (sperm). They would have more offspring because they can mate more often. The other partner puts all its resources into producing a larger gamete (egg) to ensure the survival of the offspring. This has led to the present-day division of males and females based on the kind of gametes they produce. In view of the controversy nowadays of how to define a man or a woman, difference in gamete production could be a useful way to distinguish between the two sexes.

To emancipate women from childbearing, creating an artificial womb outside the body to house the baby would be a worthy innovation. But so far, technology has failed to come up with a solution. An artificial womb remains just an idea.

The uterus is a highly sophisticated and dynamic structure whose interior is constantly changing to coincide with the monthly release of an egg from the ovaries. This cyclical transformation, the menstrual cycle, is initiated by a variety of hormones, some coming from the woman's brain, followed by others secreted by her ovaries. The uterus is not an independent entity. With such a complex sequential web of interaction, it is not surprising that scientists have not been able to construct a working replica of the human uterus.

Throughout the ages, from antiquity to the present day, the womb has been regarded as the ultimate symbol of motherhood. It is a unique female organ dedicated to childbearing. There is no male equivalent. The womb has acquired an iconic status in female biology, shrouded in myths and legends. Lana Thompson gives us an entertaining overview in *The Wandering Womb: A Cultural History of Outrageous Beliefs About Women.*

One would have thought that the possession of such a vital structure involved in procreation would enhance the image of women. But no. What should have been an asset has become a liability. In the patriarchal society of Ancient Greece, the womb was regarded disdainfully as nothing more than just a receptacle for the male sperm. It was a 'field' whose sole purpose was to nurture the developing 'seed' sown by the male.

Worse than being considered merely as an inconsequential part of the female anatomy, the womb had actually been accused of having a positively malign influence on women. Physicians in Ancient Egypt believed that many diseases in women were caused by displacement of the womb within the abdomen. This was recorded in the Kahun and Ebers papyri dating back to 1900 BC.

Greek philosophers subsequently extended this idea. Plato (429–347 BC) depicted the womb wandering inside a woman's body, creating havoc wherever it went. Aretaeus of Cappadocia, a contemporary of Galen in the 2nd century, envisaged a situation in which the womb moved too far upwards from its normal position low down in the abdomen and encroached onto the blood vessels of the head and neck, compressing them. The woman might faint or succumb to epileptic fits. These are symptoms of what we now call hysteria.

The Greek word for womb is *hustera*. Thus, the condition of hysteria got its name from its association with the womb. This Greek root for womb is preserved as prefix to many other words referring to this organ, such as *hysterectomy*, the surgical removal of the womb.

Since an artificial womb is unlikely to be available anytime soon, has modern technology anything else to offer? Surgeons are offering womb transplants. The surgical procedure is well established. The decision now is whether to use wombs from live donors or from cadavers. Spare wombs are difficult to come by so scientists are experimenting with bioengineered wombs or creating 'humanoid' wombs in animals for transplanting into humans. One day, we could find ourselves emerging from a womb constructed from a chimeric animal!

Womb transplant is a major surgical undertaking. Will there be sufficient demand for such a risky venture? Meanwhile, borrowing a womb, surrogacy, is likely to remain a popular solution.

Surrogacy is not a new idea. Hermann Muller, the American Nobel Laureate geneticist, advocated this practice in his book *Out of the Night*, back in 1935, as a way to enable women 'of good genetic stock' to produce children without having to go through the inconvenience of pregnancy themselves.

Besides the biological problem of lacking 'self' maternal genes as in egg donation described in Chapter 1, surrogacy can lead to complex legal issues. For instance, what is the nationality of the child if the commissioning couple and the surrogate are from different countries?

In Margaret Atwood's bestselling novel *The Handmaid's Tale*, the narrator is a young woman named Offred, living in an imagined future republic of Gilead. She and others like her are designated as child bearers for wives of high-ranking officials so that these wives are freed from having to go through the process of pregnancy. Offred is essentially a 'living womb'.

The Handmaid's Tale is another dystopian vision of authoritarian state control. It is not about creating new life in the laboratory as in *Brave New World*, but is a fictitious account of the enforced use of a woman's womb for procreation. Some reviewers have coined the term *speculative fiction* for stories like *The Handmaid's Tale* in that the events are not entirely fantasy but are plausible if social conditions were to change.

The different ways that surrogacy can be used appear to be unlimited. There is news of a mother acting as a surrogate to gestate a donated egg fertilised by her gay son's sperm. She gave birth to a boy who is, therefore, biologically her own grandson. Meanwhile, her gay son is now the proud father of a baby boy as well as having acquired a new brother.

'A woman gives birth to her own brother,' headed another article in the media. This is a report of a daughter acting as surrogate for her mother who has had a hysterectomy. Even the combined inventive minds of Huxley and Atwood could not have imagined that the womb can be used in so many ways. Real life is giving science fiction a run for its money. Where will it end?

Science has enriched our lives in many areas. Improving the efficiency of human reproduction is one example where technology is making significant contributions. Compared to other placental mammals, human pregnancy is the most complex because we have unique requirements that have to be met. Through trial and error, over millions of years, our mode of reproduction has adapted to constant changes in the environment. It is still a work in progress and might appear to be rather inefficient and wasteful. But this is Nature's way to balance costs and benefits to ensure that the next generation is fit to carry on our legacy. Interfering with this process for short-term gain might not be in the best interest of our species. We should regard technology as a form of repair to faults in our current reproductive system rather than as a replacement.

Human reproduction is heading towards unknown territory. We are the only species who has the technical knowledge to bypass Nature and chart our own course into the future. What will the future hold? Will it be a utopian dream or a dystopian nightmare?

11. Pandemic

As I write, the UK is at the epicentre of the COVID-19 pandemic with the dubious distinction of having the highest infection and mortality rate among all the European nations. The virus is reaping a grim toll.

The UK government allowed the virus to spread in order to create 'herd immunity'. Most of those who survive will be the young and healthy while the old and weak will succumb. It can be argued that this Darwinian selection of survival of the fittest is what Mother Nature herself would do. Nevertheless, it is a harsh government policy. Since Penny and I are in our late 80s, it is a bit scary to be pushed out as sacrificial lambs.

We are told to lock ourselves in and to avoid contact with the outside world where the virus is lurking. We have become prisoners in our own home, a surreal and eerie experience. Our lives are on hold. Time seems to stand still. We have lost track of the days of the week and even the months are hard to remember. We listen to the news to pick up what's happening outside. It's like sitting in a train watching the scenery flit by beyond the window.

During the lockdown, we are lucky to be buffered against the stress of total isolation. We live in a spacious Georgian house surrounded by sixteen acres of meadow and woodland, with two rivers running through our garden creating an island beyond the house.

The house is clad in Boston Ivy that turns from green in the summer to scarlet as the year draws to a close. 'Like the autumn leaf, burnt bright before it falls.' The wood is carpeted by white snowdrops in winter and yellow buttercups come into view in the meadow in May. The scenery is constantly changing.

By the river, between two centuries-old cedar trees, stands a beautiful Judas tree with its prolific display of deep pink flowers emerging in spring. Legend has it that Judas hanged himself from such a tree after he betrayed Jesus.

The tree in our garden has its own back story. Twenty years ago it was dying, being suffocated by the aggressive growth of ivy clambering all over its branches. Around that time, an event

Manor House in summer

Manor House in autumn

occurred that put me into a state of deep depression. I embarked on the usual regime of medication.

I am lucky my daughter Amanda talked me out of it. 'Dad, you don't want to become dependent on drugs. You should take charge of your own life. Do something that will take your mind off things.' I did.

Armed with a pair of secateurs and a handsaw, I went round our garden and wood, freeing all the trees choked by ivy. The Judas tree is one of the ones I rescued. Today, both the tree and I are free to move forward with our lives without being burdened by the past. The tree is now healthy and will continue to flower long after I'm gone.

Daughters Tracey and Imogen live close by. They order food and other household essentials online to be delivered and drive us to medical appointments when required. Without their help, Penny and I would be stranded. The pandemic has made us value the importance of family ties.

Vaccines are now available and the elderly are given priority. The government proposes to identify those individuals who have been vaccinated. They will then be the first to be released from the lockdown restrictions and resume their normal lives. A vaccination certificate will become a passport to freedom. Penny and I hope we can then take tentative steps into the outside world again.

This makes me think of the 1997 film *Gattaca*, which describes a fictional future society where the population is divided into those who are genetically screened before birth and those who are conceived in the normal way. The first group called 'valids' are deemed to be superior and will qualify for professional jobs, while the second group, designated as 'invalids', are relegated to menial tasks because they are considered to be inferior, with the risk of developing inherited diseases. Thus, a two-tier hierarchy is created within the community based on genetic selection. A similar discrimination might occur based on COVID-19 vaccination.

Vaccine sceptics are disseminating misinformation about the dangers of the COVID-19 vaccine. One that caught my eye as a placenta biologist is that the vaccine can cause infertility in wo-

Imogen with Humphrey

men. They claim that the antibodies generated against the virus could inadvertently cross-react with an essential placenta protein known as Sycytin-1, thereby disrupting the proper development of the placenta. This is false. There is no structural similarity between Sycytin-1 and the COVID-19 virus. The antibodies cannot bind to both.

The origin of Sycytin-1 is a fascinating story. Since the dawn of time, humans have regularly been infected by viruses, just as we are today. Many cause serious diseases like COVID-19. Viruses do not have the necessary machinery to replicate themselves. They have to 'borrow' the genetic mechanism of the host cell they have infected by inserting their own genes into the genes of the host. Once new viral particles are formed, they come out of the cell to infect other cells and, ultimately, other individuals. This is how a virus spreads.

Sometimes, the viral genes become integrated into the DNA of the host cell and are passed down to the next and subsequent generations. When the human genome was first analysed, scientists were astonished to find that approximately 5 per cent of the human genome is made up of viral genes. We are part human, part virus!

Some of the viral genes continue to produce viral proteins. One such protein is Syncytin-1, which biologists believe is responsible for the development of the placenta. The idea that the evolution of our placental form of reproduction originated from a viral infection way back in our ancestral past might seem improbable, but there are other similar examples of what biologists term *endosymbiosis* (living together inside the same cell).

When plants first colonised our planet, they were not green. They became green when tiny granules appeared inside their cells called *chloroplasts* which were originally bacteria that had infected primitive plants during their early life on Earth. These bacteria enabled the plants to *photosynthesise*, converting carbon dioxide into oxygen in the presence of sunlight. Because these bacteria were so useful, they were permanently incorporated into the plant cells and became chloroplasts, both living together happily ever after. Now, all green plants obtain their energy by photosynthesis.

The emergence of photosynthesizing green plants had a dramatic knock-on effect on the Earth's atmosphere. The resulting accumulation of oxygen in the air led to the evolution of new oxygen-breathing life forms, the *aerobic* organisms like ourselves gradually replacing the previous *anaerobic* ones.

To make this transition, we have to put in place a mechanism to use oxygen as a form of respiration. This brings us to another example of endosymbiosis. Inside all animal cells today are small particles called mitochondria that will convert oxygen into energy for the cell. Again, like chloroplasts in plants, mitochondria were once bacteria that were incorporated into animal cells in the beginning of life on Earth and eventually became permanent residents.

While the vaccine protesters' claim is false, I am impressed by their deep understanding of placenta biology. By focussing on

Syncytin-1, they have cloaked their misinformation with a veneer of scientific credibility.

Should pregnant mothers and those who are breastfeeding be vaccinated? In my opinion, yes, they should. Antibodies are readily transferred from mother to baby in the womb during pregnancy. The human placenta is designed for this task. There are special receptors on its surface which will bind to the antibodies facilitating their transport across. Maternal antibodies are also secreted into breast milk.

The human offspring is very fortunate in having protection from maternal antibodies *before* birth, via transfer across the placenta, and also *after* birth, in milk. This is a critical period when the baby is most vulnerable as it leaves the relatively sheltered intrauterine environment for the harsher world outside.

Antibodies have been found in the cord blood of infants born to mothers infected with COVID-19, so transmission does occur in natural infections. We can assume that antibodies produced by the pregnant mother after vaccination will be similarly transported across to protect the baby in the womb.

Studies on the seasonal flu vaccine have shown that infants born to vaccinated mothers are less likely to come down with flu than those born to mothers who did not receive the vaccine. The Royal College of Obstetricians and Gynaecologists encourages pregnant women to take up the flu vaccine in winter. This advice should be applicable to the COVID-19 vaccine.

Some patients continue to suffer from long-term debilitating symptoms after they have recovered from the acute phase of COVID-19. This happens also in some other infections. To illustrate this point, I said in one of my lectures, 'A patient might die during the initial phase of an acute infection. But what is even worse ...' Before I could finish my sentence, howls of laughter erupted from the audience. At first, I was puzzled by the disruption but then I suddenly realised what I had said. What can be worse than death itself! They are an alert lot, these students, waiting to pounce on any slight mistake the lecturer makes.

Epidemics and pandemics have devastated populations throughout human history. COVID-19 is just the latest culprit. We have had SARS (2003), MERS (2012), Ebola (2014) and Zika

(2015), stretching back to the Black Death in the Middle Ages. And we should not forget AIDS. It is notable that all these started as zoonoses, infecting animals before establishing human-human transmission. COVID-19 is said to have started in bats. It is likely we will see further examples of zoonotic infections in future as humans and animals come into increasingly close contact.

Not all zoonoses are random transmissions. Some are highly sophisticated with humans becoming part of the lifecycle of the infective organism. These are known as *cyclo-zoonoses*. The beef and pork tapeworms are good examples.

The adult worms of both species live in the human intestine where they lay eggs which are passed in faeces. These eggs, when swallowed by a cow or pig, develop in the flesh of these animals. The cycle is completed when humans eat insufficiently cooked beef or pork. Beware of steak tartare! A major difference between these two worms is that the eggs of the beef tapeworm are infective only to a cow, whereas eggs from the pork tapeworm are infective to both pig and human, making the latter a much more dangerous disease. The eggs of the pork tapeworm, when ingested by humans, can cause serious damage when they become embedded in the patient's tissues.

I once asked a candidate in an exam, 'If you have the choice, which tapeworm would you rather have, beef or pork?'

'I would definitely choose beef tapeworm,' he answered immediately. I was impressed by his quick response and asked him why.

'I will be in deep trouble if I get pork tapeworm because I am a Muslim!'

Religious rituals, such as avoiding beef or pork, could have originated from observations of these parasitic infections.

Dog lovers might be disappointed to learn that their favourite pets are potential sources of several zoonotic infections. Dog faeces may contain eggs of the dog tapeworm, which when ingested by humans can cause the serious condition known as *hydatid disease*. The worm is normally transmitted between dogs and sheep. Humans are caught up in the lifecycle when they come into close contact with these animals.

Hence, the disease is common in sheep-rearing countries like Wales, Australia or New Zealand. This is another example of a cyclo-zoonosis.

Dog faeces also contain eggs of the dog *roundworm* which are infectious to humans. The larval forms have been known to cause epilepsy when they migrate to the brain or blindness when they reach the eye. Preventing dogs from fouling parks and pavements is not just a social obligation, it is a public health duty.

In some countries, dogs are reservoirs of the protozoan parasite *Leishmania*, the cause of *leishmaniasis* in humans, transmitted by the sandfly. The diagnosis and treatment of all infected individuals can reduce the disease in a population, but if there is an animal reservoir, the spread of the disease will be more difficult to control. Many countries where leishmaniasis is endemic, such as China, have banned dogs from urban areas. Let us hope that dogs cannot transmit COVID-19.

And then there is rabies, transmitted by the bite of a rabid dog. With all these revelations, the image of the dog as 'man's best friend' is somewhat tarnished. When I pointed this out in my zoonosis lectures, it frequently drew boos and hisses from the canine-loving fraternity in the audience. I console myself that at least I have their attention.

This kind of spontaneous two-way interaction between lecturer and audience will soon be no more. Since the start of the pandemic, all lectures are now online and are likely to remain so into the future. Undoubtedly, this is highly efficient and time-saving. Once the lectures are videoed and recorded, they can be disseminated to a wide audience. And the students can access them whenever they wish. In-person lectures are no longer thought to be educationally necessary.

This is a pity. Listening to a lecture sitting alone in front of a computer screen, devoid of any personal contact with either the lecturer or other students in the lecture hall, cannot be an engaging experience. For the lecturer, too, without the buzz of a live audience, something is lost.

On Friday, 23 September 2022, after three years of isolation, I went to a college social event for the first time since the pandemic began. The occasion was a student reunion for the class of 1972.

Fifty years is a significant milestone for them and coincidentally also for me. These were the first batch of students I taught. They were 18-year-olds freshly arrived at King's, and I was a 38-year-old newly elected Fellow of the College who would be their Director of Studies, all of us thrown together into this unfamiliar environment, eyeing each other nervously. At first, they addressed me as 'sir', then as 'Dr Loke', and finally as 'Charlie' as our initial guarded relationship became more relaxed.

They are now on the cusp of 70 and I am at the boarding gate to my final destination. I am so glad to have had the chance to see them together again back at the place where we first met all those years ago.

12. Journey's End

Have I added value to the world or will I simply disappear without trace? When I retired, I created the Centre for Trophoblast Research (CTR) in Cambridge University to encourage future generations to study the placenta.

The idea was hatched one summer evening when five biology Fellows of King's College Cambridge were dining together in college. They were Barry Keverne (neuroscientist), Anne McLaren (embryologist), Ashley Moffett (pathologist), Azim Surani (geneticist) and me (immunologist). Although we seem to be from diverse disciplines, all of us have a common interest in the placenta. These are my friends who have had a significant influence on my decision to establish the CTR. Sadly, Anne McLaren was killed in a tragic car accident in July 2007. She was the driving force behind the project but just missed it come to fruition.

Professor The Honourable Dame Anne McLaren FRS (to give her full title) was a pioneer in the field of mammalian embryology. The scientific community has lost a towering figure. I, personally, miss her wise counsel and delightful company. She was a very dear friend.

The dinner at King's led to another significant development. Anne persuaded the Novartis Foundation to host a scientific meeting for us in their London headquarters to discuss trophoblast.

Anne chaired the meeting. In her introduction she said: 'The origin of this meeting was a rather good dinner in King's College, Cambridge. Since the definition of the word "trophoblast" clearly means "original feeding tissue" it is perhaps appropriate that the meeting had its origins in a good dinner!'

The above two examples serve to counter the view held by some that conversation at college High Table dinners is nothing more than just inconsequential gossip. Serious developments do emerge from time to time.

The proceedings of the Novartis meeting were published by Cambridge University Press in *Biology and Pathology of Trophoblast*, edited by Moffett, Loke and McLaren. This volume will remind me of our time together delving into the mysteries of the placenta.

Of interest to motor racing fans, Anne's family founded the company which builds the famous McLaren Formula One racing cars that competed successfully over the years against the might of Mercedes and Ferrari. Road-going models are available but they will set you back over half a million pounds each. Knightsbridge in London is a prime neighbourhood to spot one of these exotic creatures, usually driven by a Middle Eastern billionaire.

The CTR formally came into being at 4 pm Friday, 9 November 2007 when 'Report of the General Board on establishment of a Trophoblast Research Fund was graced by the University'. In plain English, this means the University has accepted my endowment for the Centre.

Trophoblast is the cell that gives the placenta its unique properties. After discussion with the School of Biological Sciences, we decided to name the Centre after this cell, leaving no doubt as to its focus. Today, the CTR is the only facility worldwide that looks exclusively at the role of the placenta in pregnancy and takes the basic science through to clinical practice.

The Centre brought together scientists from the Departments of Anatomy, Genetics, Pathology, Physiology, Obstetrics & Gynaecology as well as people from the nearby Babraham Institute and Bourn Hall Clinic. In this way, the Centre fosters interdisciplinary research across departmental boundaries. We even had someone from the Engineering Department looking at the haemodynamics of blood flow within the human placenta. Engineering science is not a discipline traditionally associated with reproductive biology.

Formation of the CTR fortuitously coincided with the merger of the University Departments of Anatomy, Physiology and Neuroscience into a single department in 2002. With great vision and generosity, Professor William (Bill) Harris, Head of this new department, offered laboratory and office space to the fledgling CTR. Today, the CTR is housed in this department.

The University also lent its support by assigning a Professorship to be held by the Director of the CTR together with a Lectureship in Reproductive Biology. The CTR is now firmly embedded into the structure and administration of Cambridge University.

Professor Graham Burton was the Founding Director of the CTR. He retired in 2022 after 15 years at the helm, having steered the Centre into what is now an internationally renowned hub of excellence for placenta research.

An important aim of the Centre is to help young investigators onto the first rung of their research career by offering New Generation Fellowships (NGFs) that will support them for a few years until they can fly on their own.

The career trajectory of Kathy Niakan is a fine example. She came to the CTR as a junior scientist and was one of our first NGFs. She then went on to the Crick Institute in London where she made a name for herself as the first person in the UK to be allowed to edit the genome of a human embryo. From there, she has now returned to Cambridge as a Professor and the new Director of the CTR, thus completing a full circle. A heart-warming success story for her and for the CTR.

Other former NGFs have also made it into established positions. Margherita Turco, who pioneered the technique for growing trophoblast and endometrial organoids (see Chapter 10), is now Head of a laboratory in Switzerland. Erica Watson and Amanda Sferruzzi-Perri are both tenured University Lecturers in Cambridge.

And here is an email (2 June 2022) from a recent NGF who has become independent.

> Dear Charlie,
> I just wanted to say a quick thank you for supporting the NGFs. I have recently transitioned from the NGF to the MRC Career Development Award. The NGF was such a tremendous help for my career.
> Best wishes
> Irving

It is gratifying to see that the CTR has made an impact, not only on placenta research, but also on the personal lives of those doing the research. At the same time, it has also enhanced the international reputation of Cambridge University. These are the three goals we aimed to achieve when setting up the CTR: to benefit the science, the people working in the science and the place where the science is done. I think we have succeeded.

For my own college, King's, I have endowed a Loke Yew Fellowship in Medical Sciences in memory of Grandfather. I have also provided funding for a PhD Studentship to be held in the University Department of Pathology. King's and Pathology have been an integral part of my academic life. They were my 'home away from home'. These contributions are for me to say thank you.

On Wednesday, 22 July 2009, I was presented with the Chan-

Duke of Edinburgh presenting me with medal at Buckingham Palace.

cellor's 800th Anniversary Medal for Outstanding Philanthropy by the Duke of Edinburgh at Buckingham Palace. Cambridge University came into being in 1209.

Penny came with me. We felt very grand and important driving through those huge palace gates so familiar from news bulletins. The ceremony took place in a room behind the balcony where the Royals come out to wave to the crowds below. I have always wondered what lies behind there. Now I know.

When the Duke handed me the medal, he said to me: 'I don't know what you can do with this. I suppose you can always flog it.' A typical DoE remark. Yes, I can certainly 'flog it' for a good price. The medal is made from 500 g of solid silver.

Since Grandfather was one of the founders of Hong Kong University, I decided to do something there too by creating a Loke Yew Professor of Pathology in the University. Professor Irene Ng

Amanda with Vice-Chancellor of Hong Kong University presenting the Loke Yew Professorship of Pathology to Professor Irene Ng

is the first holder of the post. Besides buildings and street names, the memory of Loke Yew is now firmly established also in the academic world.

What now? Should I return to Asia and try to resuscitate my roots? I have enjoyed my stay in Cambridge, but it is time to move on.

I am aware of the difficulties I will face on re-entry into Malaysian society. I might not be able to shake off the 'impostor syndrome' and I will meet people who do not approve of the path I have taken. The environment I grew up in will no longer be the same. And many of my friends have died.

We ourselves have also changed. As Benjamin Button remarked in one of F. Scott Fitzgerald's short stories, 'It's a funny thing coming home. Nothing changes. Everything looks the same, feels the same, even smells the same. You realise what's changed is you.'

Going back takes courage but I am willing to face the challenge. My reward is I will be with my own people and in my own country where I belong. In my twilight years, a sense of belonging becomes an increasingly palpable emotion.

I am optimistic. Every time I visit Malaysia, the people I meet are hospitable and friendly. 'Welcome home' is the usual greeting. It is not just 'welcome' but 'welcome HOME'. The addition of this single word is meaningful. They still think of me as a fellow Malaysian despite my long absence and not as someone just passing through. This is encouraging.

Clive James, the late Australian author and broadcaster from Sydney who, like me, had spent most of his life in Britain, had been too ill to return to Australia but was sustained by vivid recollections of his homeland. The last lines of his poem 'Sentenced to Life' resonate with me:

> Here in the English autumn, but my mind
> Basks in the light I never left behind.

I too have a light I never left behind. Is the light I left behind a true reflection of the Malaysia of today? Is it a rose-tinted image? Reading *A Malaysian Journey* by the journalist Rehman Rashid makes me pause. His vivid account of the country is different from how I remembered it to be all those years ago. Much has changed; some things for the better while others less so. And there is now a new generation of Malaysians. Going home will be quite an adventure.

Clive James chose autumn as the period when his mind turned to home. Before I retired, autumn used to be my favourite time of year. It heralded the beginning of a new academic year with the arrival of a fresh group of students. College reopened after a long summer break. There was a general air of purposeful excitement.

But now, autumn merely represents the end of summer and the start of winter. The nights are drawing in and there is a chill in the air. The mood is more sombre. It is time for me to look ahead to a Malaysian future and leave behind an English past.

If I return to Malaysia, my life will come full circle. There is a satisfying sense of symmetry to end in the same place where one began.

But Penny thinks she is now too old and frail to contemplate another major upheaval. She has followed me dutifully from Europe to Asia and back again. I cannot continue to drag her around the world.

My decision to return home is put on hold for now. I don't know how my story will end. Maybe I have to prepare myself for a different ending. I am someone who likes life to be tidy and predictable. But real life is not like that. There will always be loose ends.

Epilogue

In the midst of this pandemic, the present is so grim and the future uncertain that visiting the past can be a rich and rewarding experience. While I write, I am transported into another world. Only now have I seriously begun to examine my life. As Jordan Peterson says in *12 Rules for Life*, 'You must determine where you have been in your life, so that you can know where you are now.'

There is no better time for self-reflection than during this enforced period of inactivity. In 1820, the poet John Keats wrote his memoir under similar circumstances while quarantined aboard a ship anchored off the Bay of Naples because the disease, typhus, was raging in the city.

'You should not suppose you know the story of your life until it's over,' warns Howard Jacobson in *Live a Little*. Who then will tell my story? I want to claim my own narrative before fading memories are lost forever. By writing it down, I hope to make sense of the events that have shaped my life.

The customary neutral style of science writing which I am used to strips away all the author's personality. My job then is to transmit information, not my feelings. In a memoir, I can allow my imagination full flow and my own voice to be heard.

I have enjoyed putting my life on the page and seeing it turned into a story. It is a simple account of how a boy from a far-off tropical island became a don in Cambridge University. At its heart is a personal journey into the world of academia and scientific research. It is not a tale of redemption nor one of deprived childhood. My background, in fact, is comfortable and privileged.

Many memoirs these days are personal accounts of trauma, grief and despair, with a matching increase in appetite for books about the misery of others. I hope my memoir will redress the balance: life doesn't always have to be bleak but can be an uplifting experience.

But a life without struggle might be difficult to portray. As the French author Henry de Montherlant elegantly put it, 'Happiness writes in white ink on white paper.' Without narrative drama, a story can disappear without trace.

Nevertheless, we need to record and preserve our own stories no matter how mundane because each individual experience is different and deserves to be told. We do not have to be a celebrity. Even an ordinary life has meaning.

I have not shared everything. Some things are best left unsaid either because they can be hurtful to others or I simply wish to keep certain events of my life to myself. But there are no 'untruths'. I have told no lies.

Readers nowadays are extremely sensitive about issues such as 'identity theft', 'lived experience' or 'cultural appropriation'. A memoir should be relatively safe. I tell my own story and not someone else's. But it would be wise not to leave any skeletons in the closet as we see in the following tale.

The black comedy *Kind Hearts and Coronets* tells the story of Louis D'Ascoyne Mazzini who killed off several of his relatives, the murders so cleverly disguised as accidents that he was never under suspicion. However, his life unravelled one day when he was falsely accused and convicted for the murder of a friend, Lionel Holland, and jailed for a crime he did not commit.

While awaiting his fate in prison, he unburdened himself by writing his memoir, detailing the ingenious ways he bumped off his relatives. The day before his execution, new evidence revealed that Lionel, in fact, had committed suicide and was not murdered. Louis was reprieved. As he walked away free from the prison gate, he realised with panic that he had left his incriminating memoir behind in his prison cell for all to see.

My story spans 80 years, bookended between World War II and the present COVID pandemic. I was 7 years old when the Japanese occupied Malaya, and I am now 87 living in lockdown Britain. Looking back over this period, it is more like a dream than a memory.

Bibliography

Amis, Kingsley. *Lucky Jim*. Penguin Classics, 1954

Atwood, Margaret. *The Handmaid's Tale*. McClelland & Stewart, 1985

Austen, Jane. *Pride and Prejudice*. Penguin Classics, 1813

Cohen, Richard. *How to Write Like Tolstoy*. One World, 2016

Fairbairn, Daphne. *Odd Couples*. Princeton University Press, 2013

Forster, E.M. *A Passage to India*. Penguin Classics, 1924

Fauser, Bart and Devroey, Paul, *Baby-Making*. Oxford University Press, 2011

Gordon, Richard. *Doctor in the House*. Michael Joseph, 1952

Gunesekera, Romesh. *Suncatcher*. The New Press, 2019

Harari, Yuval Noah. *Sapiens: A Brief History of Humankind*. Random House, 2011

Hughes, Thomas. *Tom Brown's School Days*. Macmillan, 1857

Huxley, Aldous. *Brave New World*. Chatto & Windus, 1932

Ishiguro, Kazuo. *Remains of the Day*. Faber & Faber, 1989

Jacobson, Howard. *Live a Little*. Jonathan Cape, 2019

James, Clive. *Sentenced to Life*. Picador/Macmillan, 2015

Khoo, Joo Ee. *The Straits Chinese: A Cultural History*. The Pepin Press, 1996

Khor, Neil. *Loke Yew: A Malayan Pioneer*. Zamilyn Sdn Bhd, 2019

Loke, Y.W. *Immunology and Immunopathology of the Human Foetal-Maternal Interaction*. Elsevier/North Holland, 1978

Loke, Y.W. *Life's Vital Link: The Astonishing Role of the Placenta*. Oxford University Press, 2013

Loke, Y.W. and King, Ashley. *Human Implantation, Cell Biology and Immunology*. Cambridge University Press, 1995

Maugham, Somerset. *Lisa of Lambeth*. Fisher Unwin, 1897

Moffett, Ashley, Loke, Charlie, McLaren, Anne, eds. *Biology and Pathology of Trophoblast*. Cambridge University Press, 2006

Muller, Hermann. *Out of the Night: A Geneticist's View of the Future*. Vanguard, 1935

Murray, Douglas. *The Madness of Crowds: Gender, Race and Identity*. Bloomsbury 2019

Naipaul, V.S. *An Area of Darkness*. André Deutsch, 1964

Pattenden, Rosemary. *Greta Burkill: Mother to Thousands*. Peterhouse Annual Record, 2015/2016

Peterson, Jordan. *12 Rules for Life*. Random House Canada, 2018

Rashid, Rehman. *A Malaysian Journey*. Rahman Rashid, 1993

Rentzenbrink, Cathy. *Write It All Down: How to Put Your Life Down on the Page*. Bluebird, 2022

Roy, Arundhati. *The God of Small Things*. Harper Collins, 1997

Thompson, Lana. *The Wandering Womb: A Cultural History of Outrageous Beliefs About Women*. Prometheus Books, 1998

Wilkinson, Patrick. *Kingsmen of a Century*. King's College Cambridge, 1980

Printed in Great Britain
by Amazon

1e3d131b-6654-48cb-b0f7-8d231fec25a9R01